MW00714751

HALTON SKETCHES REVISITED

Historical Tales
of People and Events
in North Halton

John McDonald

The BOSTON
MILLS PRESS

This book is dedicated to my mother,
Dorothy Elizabeth (Service) McDonald.

A BOSTON MILLS PRESS BOOK

Published by Boston Mills Press, 2003
132 Main Street, Erin, Ontario N0B 1T0
Tel: 519-833-2407   Fax: 519-833-2195
e-mail: books@bostonmillspress.com
www.bostonmillspress.com

In Canada:
Distributed by Firefly Books Ltd.
3680 Victoria Park Avenue
Toronto, Ontario M2H 3K1

In the United States:
Distributed by Firefly Books (U.S.) Inc.
P.O. Box 1338, Ellicott Station
Buffalo, New York 14205

Copyright © John McDonald, 1996, 2003

National Library of Canada Cataloguing in Publication

McDonald, John (John Robert)
    Halton sketches revisited : historical tales of people and places / John McDonald. —
1st Boston Mills Press ed.

First ed. published 1976 under title: Halton sketches.

ISBN 1-55046-375-6

1. Halton Hills (Ont.)—History. 2. Halton Hills (Ont.)—Biography.
3. Halton (Ont.) History. 4. Halton (Ont.)—Biography. I. Title.

FC3095.H345M32 2003   971.3'533   C2002-901525-1
F1059.H28M37 2003

Printed in Canada

COVER ILLUSTRATION:
'MEET ME AT THE STATION' WAS OFTEN HEARD IN GEORGETOWN AFTER THE RAILROAD
LINE WAS BUILT THROUGH THE VILLAGE IN 1856. TRAVELLING SALESMEN, VISITING RELA-
TIVES, AND SUNDAY SCHOOL PICNICS ARRIVED AND DEPARTED FROM THE STATION. IN THIS
PHOTOGRAPH WILLOUGHBY'S UNION BUS AND A CROWD WAIT FOR A TRAIN IN 1910.

TITLE PAGE ILLUSTRATION:
MESSRS. ROBERTSON AND LAIDLAW BUILT THE TWO ORIGINAL LIME KILNS AT DOLLY
VARDEN IN 1872. DR. MCGARVIN AND C.S. SMITH OF ACTON OWNED THE CANADA LIME
WORKS WHEN THIS SKETCH FROM COMPANY STATIONERY WAS USED IN THE EARLY 1880'S.

The terms "Concession" and "Line" are used interchangeably throughout
the text as both terms are still in current use. In the original surveys the
approximately north-south roads were designated Concession Lines. The
approximately east-west roads were termed Side Roads.

Contents

INTRODUCTION

When, as editor of *The Georgetown Independent*, I first approached John McDonald about writing a series of articles on the families of Halton Hills in May of 1974, little did either of us anticipate they would expand into a volume. However, the first edition of *Halton Sketches*, composed of newspaper columns from *The Independent* and *The Acton Free Press*, appeared in 1976, published by Dills Printing and Publishing Company Limited, proprietors of the newspapers.

The popularity of the series and the demand for a book encompassing the articles grew as they appeared. The information entrusted to the author, some of it sensitive, was a tribute to the trust given to him. His accuracy in dealing with family histories probably brought out more family information than might ordinarily have appeared. Handled awkwardly the information could have embarrassed some of our first families, rather than weaving a tapestry of their various backgrounds.

In his quest for first-hand evidence John winnowed mounds of chaff gleaned from local stories, family diaries and notebooks, folklore, newspaper clippings and interviews. This entailed long hours, much travel and endless poking into family closets, unsure some-times whether they may have contained skeletons better left uncovered.

John's flesh and blood approach to each chapter, rather than dealing with bricks and mortar subjects, provided fascinating insights into the past. The preservation of timber and rust-worn metal he has left to others. He has kept the memory of men and women who built the foundations for our way of life ever green. Understandably there were just too many stories to deal with in one volume, hence this updated and expanded edition of *Halton Sketches*.

Unlike many glimpses into history, this edition is copiously illustrated with photographs to bring the stories alive. The character of the subjects can often be read in the unforgiving studio portraits of the 19th century.

This edition of *Halton Sketches* is a welcome key to the past. It is also a resource book which I'm sure many people will study with the enthusiasm it merits. Let us also hope the author's prolific pen has the capacity for yet another volume.

Hartley Coles,
April, 1996

PREFACE

The first edition of *Halton Sketches* was never meant to be a concise history of the north Halton area of Ontario, as it was based on a series of articles I had written for *The Georgetown Independent* and *The Acton Free Press* newspapers. *Halton Sketches* did, however, provide a glimpse of some of the early entrepreneurs of the area with an emphasis on not only their accomplishments but their family life and their contribution to the community.

Halton Sketches first appeared in book form in 1976 and went out-of-print in the early 1980's. After some encouragement from people who had written to me over the years, and in particular Norman Holt (owner of Oxbow Books), I decided that an updated edition on the occasion of *Halton Sketches'* twentieth anniversary would be appropriate.

I want to thank those who appear in the Acknowledgements for their kind assistance with the first edition, and in many instances helping me update the information for this revision. Their friendship has been most treasured.

John McDonald
September, 1996

Halton Historical Overview

The Regional Municipality of Halton is situated strategically at the western end of Lake Ontario between Toronto and Hamilton and close to the United States border. Approximately 45 kilometres long and 24 kilometres wide, it is bounded by Lake Ontario to the south, Peel Region on the east, Wentworth County on the west and Wellington County on the north.

In the late 1700's and early 1800's when surveys and pioneer settlements were in their infancy in southern Ontario, the numerous river mill sites, rich agricultural land and abundance of raw materials, such as timber and lime, made Halton prosperous.

Halton, one of the oldest counties in Canada, was named after Major William Mathew Halton. An Englishman, he was the son of Sir William and Lady Halton. In 1799 he was gazetted as a Major in the Fencible Cavalry and appears to have sold his commission in 1801, but continued to be unofficially called Major. While in England in 1805, Halton was named Secretary to the Upper Canada provincial Lieutenant-Governor Sir Francis Gore. He arrived in Upper Canada the following year. He returned to England in 1811 but came back to Canada in 1815.

In 1816 Halton was named to the newly created position of Provincial Agent in England by Gore. Records indicate that he wanted to go back to 'the old country'. He acted as Provincial Agent from 1816 to 1821 and never returned to Upper Canada. His tenure irritated the establishment in Upper Canada because of his constant pressuring for some form of compensation or land grants for those loyal citizens of Upper Canada who had defended the province during the 1812 war against the Americans. In a letter dated August 25, 1818, Halton stated that Americans had "long ago" received remuneration from their government for losses during the war and were in full view across the Niagara River of the loyalists in Upper Canada. Some felt that Halton's view was handicapped by being out of touch with conditions in the province. The Provincial Agent in England position itself had been a matter of much controversy since its inception and was finally abolished in 1822.

Soon after his return to England in 1816, Halton's health began to fail. Records show that even though his health had completely broken down by 1821, he did attempt to continue his duties. After a long illness Halton, the man after whom this region was named, died on September 22, 1821 in London.

Before the coming of the earliest immigrants to north Halton, the area was populated mainly by Missisauga Indians.

Settlers started to arrive in what we know as the Halton area in the early 1780's and they found a dense forest of mostly hardwood and pine. The first transportation routes were the waterways, with only Indian trails through the forest linking them. The south part of what is now Halton was first settled by United Empire Loyalists from across the United States border. The northern part of Halton was settled mainly by immigrants from the British Isles as evidenced by such areas as 'the Scotch Block' and the 'English Block' in Esquesing Township.

The first municipal organization of what is now the Province of Ontario was created on July 24, 1788 when Lord Dorchester, Governor-In-Chief of British North America issued a proclamation dividing Upper Canada into four districts: Lunenburgh, Mecklinburgh, Nassau and Hesse. Each had its own individual system comprised of sheriff, judges and coroners and eventually courthouse and jail.

The Provincial Act of 1792 renamed the four districts Eastern, Midland, Home and Western. Halton formed a part of the Home District. By 1816 Halton and Wentworth Counties made up the newly formed Gore District. Halton contained the townships of Beverley, Dumfries and Esquesing. According to the *Atlas of the County of Halton* the population of the Gore District had reached 6 684 in 1817. The majority were United Empire Loyalists. The Crown Survey Act (also of 1792) required townships be surveyed prior to the arrival of new settlers.

Halton and Wentworth counties were reduced to their present size in 1832 but remained united until 1853. Thompson's Inn in the village of Milton was the site of the first (provisional) County Council Meeting on July 12, 1853. Full municipal and judicial powers were granted to Halton on January 1, 1855.

Halton comprised four townships: Trafalgar (named after the famous battle), Nelson (after Viscount Horatio

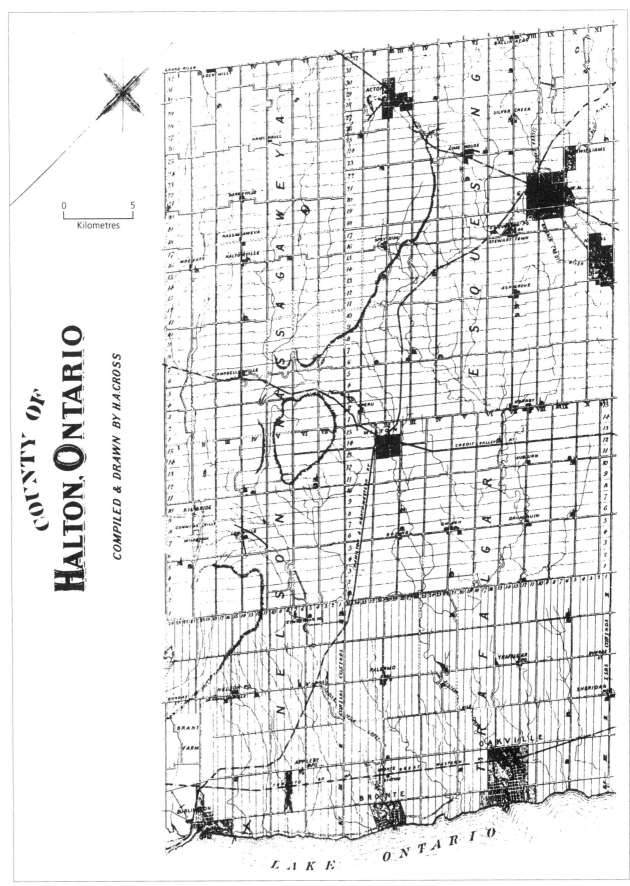

HALTON COUNTY, AS DEPICTED IN THE 1877 *ATLAS OF THE COUNTY OF HALTON*.

Nelson), Nassagaweya (Missisauga Indian word for the river "having two outlets"), and Esquesing. There has been controversy concerning the meaning of the Indian word "Esquesing". Some claim this is the Missisauga name for "last out creek" while others argue it refers to "land of the tall pine".

By 1857 both Milton and Oakville were incorporated as towns in the County of Halton. Georgetown became incorporated as a village in 1865, while Burlington and Acton became villages in 1873 and 1874 respectively.

This book mainly deals with Georgetown, Acton, Glen Williams, Limehouse and Norval. These areas of settlement are all located in what was called until recently the Township of Esquesing. Each had excellent mill sites on the waterways which wind through the area to Lake Ontario, and all are surrounded by very rich agricultural land. The Niagara Escarpment, a limestone ridge with a long gradual slope on one side and steep slope on the other, snakes through the western part of the area discussed in this book and was an important natural resource for early construction material.

The original names for most of the communities in this book have disappeared, changed usually when the local post office was opened. By the mid-1850's whether or not a railroad passed through a village had a great bearing on the industrial and commercial success of the settlement. Even though Glen Williams, Norval and Stewarttown had tremendous waterpower (hence the establishment of mills from the 1820's), it was Georgetown, Limehouse and Acton who 'won out' with the

Grand Trunk railroad line going through these communities and providing full service when the line officially opened in 1856.

The flow of transportation of people and goods from the 1820's onward was mainly north-south between these northern villages to the port of Oakville on Lake Ontario. Often material had to be hauled by teams of oxen and horses on toll roads constructed of planks. Trafalgar Road was once a major toll road through the area (which was impossible to navigate during the spring thaw!). With the advent of the railroad in the mid-1850's, the transportation flow became east-west with the shipping and receiving of goods to and from Toronto and points eastward by rail.

Once-bustling settlements, such as Limehouse, are now quaint villages where residents travel to neighbouring towns and cities for employment. Many men and women operated the lime kilns and saw mills, or worked in paint factories and woollen mills in the 1880's and 90's.

The 'capital' of the former Township of Esquesing was the village of Stewarttown on Trafalgar Road immediately south of Georgetown. The place was named after John and Duncan Stewart who settled in the area in

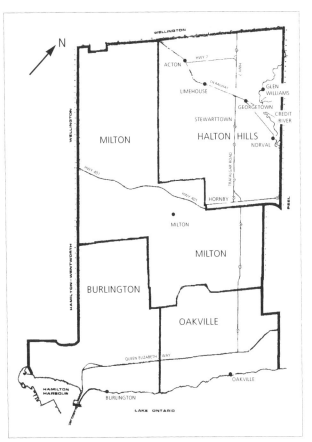

HALTON REGION.

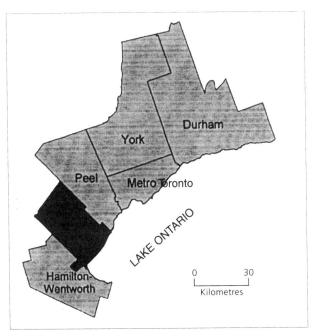

HALTON AND THE GREATER TORONTO AREA.

3

1818 and are believed to have been the first settlers in the township. The post office, which opened in 1820, was called 'Esquesing' and was the first in the area.

Stewarttown became a very active industrial site by the early 1850's, due mainly to water power from the west branch of the Credit River. The building, however, of the Grand Trunk Railway through Georgetown (and not Stewarttown) signed its fate as an important centre of commerce in north Halton. (The *Halton County Atlas* also attributes this to the fact that a "former owner of the mills was a non-resident".)

The Township of Esquesing Council met in Stewarttown from 1850 until 1963 when the council chambers moved up Trafalgar Road to a site 1 kilometre north.

Like most communities in southern Ontario the north Halton area enjoyed the boom in commerce with the industrial revolution and many of its own entrepreneurs succeeded in their respective businesses. World War One, the great depression and World War Two brought some misery to the area, with the period between the 1930's and 1950's being one of relatively slow growth. After the mid-1950's, however, the relocation of several new major national and international companies to the area, as well as the construction of Highway 401, brought a new wave of economic prosperity and citizens. This was the era when Rex Heslop developed a large tract of land to the east of Georgetown and expanded the residential and commercial aspects significantly. This new stability and growth however was threatened with the decision to close the Avro Arrow jet fighter project in nearby Malton on February 20, 1959, which employed many north Halton residents. Some area families had to abandon their new homes—and dreams—as a result of the Avro cancellation.

On January 1, 1974 the County of Halton officially became the Regional Municipality of Halton. This change of local government was met with some anguish from all sectors of the 119-year-old county. There was concern as to whether Burlington would become a part of Hamilton-Wentworth, whether Halton was going to be three or four municipalities, whether the new regional headquarters would remain in Milton, the original county seat, and of course whether each community would be able to retain its own distinct character. The Region of Halton Bill received second reading on Monday, June 18, 1973 only after several hours of heated debate which ended at 3:00 a.m. in the Legislative Assembly at Queen's Park in Toronto. On July 31, 1973 Allan Mason, Reeve of Oakville, was appointed Chairman of the new Regional Municipality of Halton by Premier William Davis. Regional headquarters eventually relocated to Oakville.

The new municipality in north Halton that we are concerned with had several interesting names proposed including Esquesing, North Halton, Actesquenassageo, Tan Town, Tall Pines and Hungry Hollow. The chosen name, of course, was Halton Hills.

Halton Hills has retained many of its unique and historic attributes and the small villages and two major urban areas have successfully retained their character. In one instance, namely Acton, some creative and successful modern entrepreneurs have developed the historic tannery and leather theme.

This brief look at north Halton from the time of early pioneers paddling down the waterways and the profiles of some of the people whose toil and enterprise built this lovely part of the province I hope will whet readers' appetites to delve further into the history of their homeland. ∞

Georgetown Historical Overview

Georgetown is situated on the Credit River about 45 kilometres from Toronto and 60 kilometres from Hamilton.

When George Kennedy, a descendant of United Empire Loyalists, established himself in the area in 1823 it was the abundant water supply for milling purposes that attracted this early entrepreneur. His mill became the beginnings of a small settlement. By 1837, however, it was reported that there were still only three families living in the area of his mill known as 'Hungry Hollow'.

It was the enterprising Barber brothers who in 1837 bought a woollen mill and foundry from Kennedy and renamed the small settlement Georgetown (presumably after George Kennedy). The Barber brothers' businesses flourished and attracted other industrialists such as the Dayfoots who arrived in the early 1840's and became pioneers in the leather and shoe trade in Ontario. It was the papermaking business, however, which the Barber brothers had operated since 1854, that became a real source of prosperity to the Georgetown community for over a century.

Just as the excellent sites for water power and ponds in the early 1820's and the opening up of the York (or Toronto) to Guelph road (now Highway 7) in 1827 helped to establish this area as a settlement location, it was the building of the Grand Trunk Railroad through Georgetown (completed in 1856) and the Hamilton and North West Railroad (completed in 1877) that confirmed Georgetown would be the centre of commerce and industry in the north Halton area.

Georgetown grew rapidly during the 1850's and 60's. By 1864 it had a population of 1 250 and the citizens decided that it would be in their best interest to "have the management of their own local affairs in the hands of men of their own choice". An application was made to Halton County Council for incorporation as a Village. This was granted on December 16, 1864. The first Reeve was James Young, a merchant in the village.

The 1860's and 70's saw further growth and prosperity. The *Georgetown Herald* newspaper was founded in 1866. Culp and Mackenzie started to build their award-winning carriages on Main Street in 1860. The Creelman brothers founded their knitting machine

LOOKING NORTH AT MAIN AND MILL STREETS, DOWNTOWN GEORGETOWN, IN THE EARLY 1900'S. THE ONLY STREET LIGHT IN THE VILLAGE HANGS OVER THE INTERSECTION.

THE GEORGETOWN TOWN HALL SAT AT THE CORNER OF BACK AND CROSS STREETS FROM 1878 UNTIL COMPLETELY DESTROYED BY FIRE IN 1968.

company in 1876. The Bank of Hamilton opened a branch office in Georgetown in 1875, the first chartered financial institution in all of Halton County.

By the 1870's and 80's the village was undergoing architectural change. Wooden frame homes and public buildings built as early as the 1840's and 50's including stores, churches and schools, were being replaced by brick and stone edifices. The new Chapel Street school and Baptist Church were both completed in 1869, the Town Hall in 1878, while the new high school—designed by prominent Toronto architect Edward Lennox—was completed in 1887. A walk around the old village of Georgetown today, looking at dates on corner stones, will confirm that the 1870's and 80's were the heyday of architecture in Georgetown.

By 1891 Georgetown had installed its first waterworks system. Springs on Silver Creek Hill were piped by gravity from approximately 5 kilometres north-west of the village.

Georgetown didn't receive its first power from Niagara Falls until 1913, but John R. Barber had commissioned in 1888 the Cleveland Brush Company to build a 60-hp motor and 100-hp generator for the Barber Paper Mill on the Credit River. This undertaking is reported to have been the first long-distance transmission of hydro-electric power for manufacturing purposes in North America.

In 1901 H. T. Arnold, a tanner, and J.B. Mackenzie, a lumber supplier, both expanded their Acton businesses to Georgetown. John A. Willoughby erected a stone building in 1906 for his livery and bus business. The building now houses Branch 120 of The Royal Canadian Legion on Mill Street. William Smith and Benny Stone joined forces in 1919 in Georgetown to produce one of the more successful lines of electrical wire devices.

MAP LEGEND

1. ARMOURY
2. FAIRGROUNDS
3. JOSEPH MOORE RESIDENCE
4. WESLEYAN METHODIST CHURCH
5. H.P. LAWSON RESIDENCE
6. MARKET SQUARE/OLD FAIRGROUNDS
7. LAWSON PLANING MILL/MACKENZIE LUMBER
8. BAPTIST CHURCH
9. LAWSON'S TROUT POND
10. BENNETT HOUSE HOTEL
11. WILLOUGHBY'S LIVERY STABLE/LEGION
12. CONGREGATIONAL CHURCH/CULTURAL CENTRE
13. KNOX PRESBYTERIAN CHURCH
14. BERWICK HALL/BARBER RESIDENCE
15. TORONTO SUBURBAN RAILWAY STATION
16. MCGIBBON HOTEL

17. BUCK'S FINE FOODS
18. J.B. MACKENZIE RESIDENCE
19. KENNEDY/LAWSON RESIDENCE
20. BRADLEY'S CEDAR VALE FARM
21. SILVER CREEK
22. WILBER LAKE/EARLY INDUSTRY
23. TOWN HALL
24. ST. JOHN'S UNITED CHURCH
25. CHAPEL STREET PUBLIC SCHOOL
26. HOLY ROSARY/SACRÉ COEUR CATHOLIC CHURCH
27. BUCK RESIDENCE
28. MEMORIAL ARENA
29. BUCK'S ABATTOIR/LION'S POOL
30. DAYFOOT RESIDENCE
31. DAYFOOT SHOE FACTORY
32. ARNOLD GLOVE WORKS

33. SAXE CREAMERY
34. ST. GEORGE'S ANGLICAN CHURCH
35. GEORGE KENNEDY HOMESTEAD
36. GEORGETOWN DISTRICT HIGH SCHOOL
37. JACK TOST FARM
38. SMITH AND STONE FACTORY
39. GRAND TRUNK/CANADIAN NATIONAL RAILROAD STATION
40. HARRY WRIGHT'S EXCHANGE HOTEL
41. H.T. ARNOLD RESIDENCE
42. DOMINION SEED HOUSE
43. CANADA COATED PAPER MILLS/ABITIBI
44. GEORGETOWN COATED PAPER MILLS/DOMTAR
45. BARBER PAPER MILLS
46. EDWARD FLECK RESIDENCE

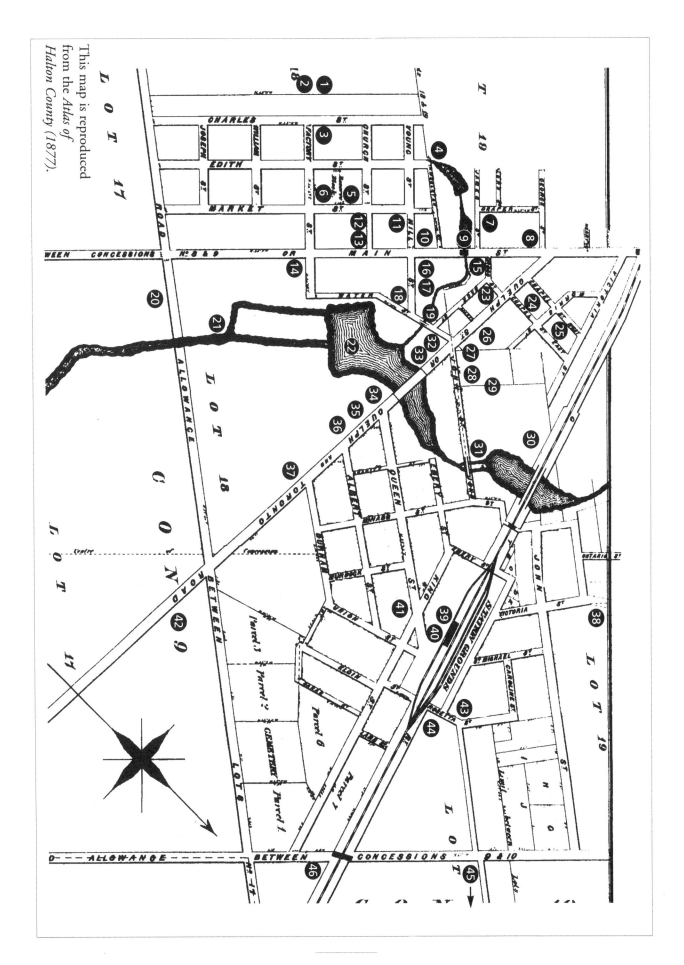

This map is reproduced from the *Atlas of Halton County (1877)*.

New 3" Rims and Tires

We will cut down your old high Wagon Wheels, put on 3" Rims and Tires; 36" front wheel, 40" rear wheel. First-class workmanship and materials We will pick up your wheels and deliver back to your farm. WRITE FOR OUR PRICES.

We do everything in
Wagon, Sleigh and Buggy Repairing
Rubber Tires Put On

HORSESHOEING AND GENERAL BLACKSMITHING

AUTO TOP, BODY and MUD GUARD REPAIRING.

J. N. O'Neill & Son

Georgetown, Ontario

PHONE 14 — "Deal at O'Neill's"

THE ABOVE WAGON is our own make. It is built of the best materials. The low-down Handy Farm Type.

FRONT WHEELS 36"   REAR WHEELS 40"   3" TIRES
AXLES 4" x 5"   STEEL TRUSS ROD
SKEINS 3½" x 11"   SPOKES 2½"
HUBS 9½" Diameter
Bolster, Sand Board and Pole extra heavy
Well Painted, Striped and Varnished

Please let us know if you are interested. Get our Prices.

AN ADVERTISEMENT FOR J. N. O'NEILL WHO PURCHASED THE CULP & MCKENZIE BLACKSMITH SHOP IN 1898. O'NEILL ERECTED THE BUILDING AT MAIN AND WESLEYAN STREETS IN 1922 AFTER A FIRE TWO YEARS EARLIER.

By 1917 The Toronto Suburban Railway provided yet another means of transportation for passengers and goods between Toronto and Guelph. The Georgetown Station on Main Street (at the current Canada Trust site) was a familiar landmark, but the venture failed in 1931 due to the depression and the advent of the automobile, as well as the proximity to the Grand Trunk (Canadian National Railway) line.

THE BUILDING OF THE GRAND TRUNK RAILROAD LINE, WHICH OPENED IN 1856, WAS AN INCENTIVE FOR BUSINESS TO MOVE TO GEORGETOWN. THE 'IRON BRIDGE' SPANS THE CREDIT RIVER TO THE EAST OF GEORGETOWN.

By 1921 the population of Georgetown had reached over 2 000. This qualified the village to petition the County to declare itself a Town. This happened in 1922 with LeRoy Dale, a prominent lawyer in Georgetown since 1914, serving as the community's first Mayor for seven years.

The Depression and World War Two brought difficult times to Georgetown but the residents pulled together. It was during this period that the Royal Canadian Legion Branch purchased Willoughby's former livery stable on Mill Street.

In the early 1950's Rex Heslop arrived in Georgetown with his plans to expand the town with a large residential, commercial and industrial development. Construction began in 1955 and attracted some industry to Georgetown, but the industrial base did not materialize to support the local demands that accompany a growing residential area. When the federal government under John Diefenbaker decided to cancel the Avro Arrow project in nearby Malton in February, 1959, over 600 Georgetown area people became unemployed virtually overnight. In 1962 another residential subdivision development, Moore Park, was announced in the west end of Georgetown on the old Moore farm.

By 1960 Georgetown had reached a population of 10 000 and a year later the community had its own hospital. In February 1974 the first GO Train pulled

AETNA LACROSSE CLUB, 1901.

out of Georgetown. This was reminiscent of an earlier effort by the Toronto Suburban Railway to offer a Toronto passenger service for Georgetown residents. This time, however, passengers rode in efficient, streamlined, two-storey passenger cars that didn't occasionally stop at the mill ponds so the conductors could drop a fishing line and 'try their luck' as they had some 50 years before on the Radial line.

On January 1, 1974 Georgetown was absorbed into the new regional town of Halton Hills. The most significant changes in the town since then include the Georgetown South residential expansion on land once owned by Heslop and later the McLaughlin Group. Construction started in 1989 after several years of debate at the council chamber and court room. Long-term growth in the town in part awaits the proving of water capacity. The Official Plan currently sets the population service limit at 37 400. Urban Georgetown in 1996 had a population of 24 300.

Civic pride in the community grew when the old Congregational Church (built in 1877 and deeded as a free public library in 1912), became part of the town's Cultural Centre, including a library and The John Elliott Theatre which opened in October, 1981. A controversy over the location of the Halton Hills municipal building was finally resolved when the new complex opened in 1989 on Maple Avenue directly across from the North Halton Golf and Country Club.

The paper industry, so dominant in the early years of Georgetown and a source of economic stability and employment for over 130 years, ceased with the closing of Provincial Papers (originally part of the John R. Barber operation) on March 31, 1991. The Georgetown Coated Paper Company (which was opened by Edward Fleck in 1910) became part of Domtar and closed its doors in 1977. ✖

GEORGE KENNEDY (1799-1870) AFTER WHOM GEORGETOWN IS
NAMED.

MRS. GEORGE KENNEDY (ELIZABETH BEDFORD).

GEORGE KENNEDY: THE 'GEORGE' OF GEORGETOWN

Georgetown derived its name from one of the earliest pioneers in this area, George Kennedy. Some historians believe the town was named after King George III (1760-1820) but this theory has never been much supported.

George Kennedy was a descendant of United Empire Loyalists. His grandfather, John Kennedy, was born in Scotland but fled as a child to the north of Ireland during the times of religious persecution. He later settled in the United States, working for the Hudson Bay Fur Trading Company in New Jersey.

John Kennedy, the younger (George's father) was born in Sussex County, New Jersey, May 8, 1761 and became a schoolteacher. His loyalty was to the British and following the American Revolution he came to Canada on June 8, 1796. During the trip many hardships were encountered with his wife and five small children. His horses died and an infant son was captured by an Indian. After a chase the child, Morris, was rescued. John Kennedy, the younger, died April 12, 1847.

Five Kennedy brothers, John, Charles, Morris, Samuel and George arrived in the area. Charles was hired to do the earliest surveys in this part of Esquesing Township and established a saw mill on the Eighth Line north of Georgetown near Wildwood. It was George Kennedy who created the first industrial site in the area which the village grew around.

George Kennedy was born September 16, 1799, in Middleport, Gainsborough Township. He married Elizabeth Bedford on May 24, 1821, and two years later they settled in Esquesing Township.

He took up 200 acres of land from the Crown, bordering on the Check Line (Maple Avenue) on the south, extending from the Ninth Line (Mountainview Road) on the east to the Eighth Line (Main Street) on the west. The northern boundary was in the vicinity of Ewing Street.

The area was virgin forest in 1823 and Kennedy commenced to clear the land. He built the first dwelling in what was known as 'Hungry Hollow' and made his home in a log cabin near what is now St. George's Anglican Church. With the advantages of a surveying background, Kennedy began to establish a settlement. Recognising the need for mills as a basis for the new community, he built a saw and grist mill at the meeting place of two streams near the present Mill and Guelph Street intersection.

CHARLES KENNEDY'S SAWMILL LOCATED AT WILDWOOD AND THE EIGHTH CONCESSION.

Kennedy built the first brick house on Mill Street. The second brick house at 73 Mill Street, which he built for his son, was directly across the street.

In 1837 the name of the small community of only three families was changed to Georgetown in honour of its founder. 1837 is also significant because the enterprising Barber Brothers arrived and created an industrial base. It was from George Kennedy that they purchased a mill site and the rights to build a dam. Kennedy provided not only the land, but building materials on easy terms to help the Barbers get established.

The site of St. George's Anglican Church and the material for the rectory and the original church building were all a gift from George Kennedy. Maple Avenue, from Main Street to Guelph Street, was a 'given road' provided to the municipality by George Kennedy. The old Kennedy homestead is now the site of the Post Office, the former Wrigglesworth School and Georgetown District High School. Jack Tost, a descendant of Kennedy, was the last to own the farm.

George Kennedy and his wife Elizabeth had a family of nine children. Their daughter, Harriet, was the first white child born in Georgetown. George Kennedy died at 71 years of age in 1870 and is buried in Greenwood Cemetery.

Several generations of Kennedys have lived and farmed in this area. William Cyrus Kennedy (1859-1935), George's grandson, was raised on the Kennedy homestead. At the age of 15 he ran a games booth at Orangeville Fair and thus began a lifelong interest. For 61 years. he sold candy and popcorn at local fall fairs. For a short time he operated a travelling animal show which featured bears, three-legged goats, a horse with cow's feet and tail and other oddities of nature. Several neighbours complained about the unusual animal sounds when he lived downtown (near 83 Mill Street). Cyrus also operated a grocery and confectionery store in a portion of the former Buck's Fine Food building at 96 Mill Street.

The Kennedy family has contributed to the development of the town since its earliest days, George Kennedy in establishing the settlement and several descendants by serving on council and various public boards and committees after a municipal village and town were incorporated. Kennedy was a well-respected mercantile name on Georgetown's main street for many years.

George Kennedy's memory is perpetuated in a memorial cairn erected at Greenwood Cemetery and in the naming of a public school in his honour. ∞

THE BARBER BROTHERS: GEORGETOWN'S IRISH ENTREPRENEURS

John R. Barber had one of the first automobiles in Georgetown, a Russell Knight. He would invite the locals to take their horses out to the park to become familiar with the 'iron contraption' as he drove it around.

It was 1822 when the Barber family, consisting of father, mother, four sons and a daughter left County Antrim, Ireland, for the 60-day voyage to Canada. Reaching Quebec they headed up the St. Lawrence for Montreal. At the Lachine Rapids the westbound craft was a Durham boat and the passengers had to walk along the shore through bush trails. The newcomers were alarmed by the sound of grasshoppers which they took to be the hissing of snakes!

After 11 days of land and water travel they arrived at Prescott where the father, Joseph Barber, found work in his trade as a bricklayer and stone mason. When winter set in he decided to move to the Niagara peninsula and arrived there on December 12, 1822. The Barber family remained in the Niagara region for over two years.

It was about this time that William Lyon Mackenzie was criticising government through his columns in the *Colonial Advocate* because American printing paper was coming into the country duty free. He strongly urged the government to offer some incentive for the erection of a paper mill in Upper Canada. In 1825 he called a meeting in York (Toronto) and proposed that the Legislature be asked to award a $500 bounty for the first paper mill established. A petition was drawn up and subsequently an Act was passed on January 30, 1826 offering payment to the man who produced the first sheet of paper.

The race was on. James Crooks, who had an excellent mill site just east of Dundas, advertised for rags to be used in the manufacture of paper. He went to Niagara and secured Joseph Barber as stone mason to erect his mill. He also offered employment to as many of the Barber children that could work.

William and Robert Barber started in the Crooks' woollen mill, Joseph Jr. became a machinist and James worked in the paper mill. Crooks won the paper race and the bounty offered for the first sheet of paper manufactured in the province... his rivals insisted that he won only by operating his mill on a Sunday!

In 1831 Joseph Barber, the father, died at Crooks' Hollow near Dundas. Six years later the Barber brothers decided to set up a business for themselves. They

BARBER PAPER MILL ON THE CREDIT RIVER AT RIVER ROAD. THIS WAS THE FIRST PAPER MILL ON THE CONTINENT TO BE OPERATED BY HYDRO-ELECTRIC POWER.

ventured along Lake Ontario by lake boat to what is now Port Credit and walked up the Credit River looking for a suitable site for a mill.

In 1837 they bought land from George Kennedy. Georgetown at that time was known as Hungry Hollow and consisted of only three families. The Barbers established a woollen mill and a foundry, which later supplied all the iron work in the area (except bridges) for the Grand Trunk Line which was built through Georgetown between 1852 and 1856. The original woollen mill and foundry were located on what is now Park Street (formerly known as Water and Factory Streets). Silver Creek, which still runs through the area, was dammed and a mill race established for power.

In 1843 a second woollen mill was started in nearby Streetsville. Robert Barber and brother-in-law Benjamin Franklin moved there to run it.

By 1850 the Barbers were operating a woollen mill, iron foundry, machine shop and saw mill in Georgetown. In 1852, a larger woollen factory was built in Streetsville, into which the machinery of both plants was put and the Georgetown plant closed.

At the same time a Scotsman David Forbes, a papermaker, was attracted to Georgetown with the building of the Grand Trunk. He negotiated with the Barbers, who put up a building for him and rented him both power and premises on the Credit River at River Drive. Shortly thereafter Forbes found the enterprise too much and the Barbers took over the paper business.

In 1869 the four Barber brothers and their brother-in-law, after carrying on various businesses for over 32 years without a deed of partnership, decided to separate and make a settlement. William and Robert purchased the woollen business in Streetsville, Joseph and Benjamin Franklin retired and James bought the paper business.

James was the father of John Roaf Barber who eventually took control of the paper business at the time of his father's death in 1880. John R. Barber was born in Georgetown, July 5, 1841 and was educated locally. He married Francis Barclay in 1868 and a year after her death in 1899 he married another local girl, Alberta Bessey. She died in 1906.

John R. had intentions of joining the British Army and attending military school but stayed home to attend to the business. He did, however, join the Georgetown Light Infantry and the 20th Halton Rifles. In 1863 he was given a commission in the Volunteer Movement and in 1866 he helped defend the province at the Peace Bridge in Fort Erie during the Fenian uprising. He later received a medal for his part in the Fenian Raids. He retired as Honorary Major from the Halton Rifles in 1905.

The determination of John R. is illustrated when in 1871 the paper company was experiencing financial problems he went to the Bank of Hamilton, got a loan, and was able to repay it within one year.

John R. could remember the first shipment of paper to Toronto by rail. The paper was loaded on construction flat cars, as regular freight service to Toronto hadn't started. Three Barber boys, Joseph, John R. and James Jr. acted as a fire brigade because the locomotives were still burning wood and the danger of sparks setting the paper afire was very real.

John R. told the story of the night of the Great Toronto Fire of 1904 when he was in the city and helped save the Queen's Hotel building by using chamber pots to carry water to douse sparks as they landed on the roof! He also recalled that bridge warning cords

THE CANADA COATING PAPER MILL CONSTRUCTED IN 1905 WAS KNOWN AS THE 'UPPER MILL' AND IS LOCATED NEAR THE RAILROAD STATION.

WORKERS POSE AT THE CANADA COATING PAPER MILL.

for brakemen walking on the top of freight cars were first used at the Mountainview Road bridge.

In 1888 John R. recognized the need for more power at the paper mill and commissioned the Cleveland Brush Company in Ohio to build a 60 hp motor and a 100 hp generator which were apparently larger than anything he had used previously. The dynamo plant was installed over a kilometre down river from the paper mill site (due to a 7-metre drop compared to a 5-metre drop in the river at the mill site).

Ontario Hydro confirms this was the first long distance transmission of hydro-electric power for manufacturing purposes in North America. The ruins of the dynamo stand beside the Credit River as a monument to this undertaking and can be seen from the embankment at the corner of Sinclair and Armstrong Avenues.

During the 1880's John R. Barber had the large home at 139 Main Street South constructed. It was designed by the prominent architect, Edward Lennox, who also designed the old Toronto City Hall and the King Edward Hotel. The residence was named 'Berwick Hall' after the birthplace of his mother, Hannah Patrick, who was born at Berwick-on-Tweed, England.

John R. lived there until his death March 3, 1917. His eldest son Frank took over the estate but moved out in 1918 and the building sat idle for many years and was known as a 'haunted house' for a generation of Georgetown children. In 1945 Bill Bradley, founder of the Dominion Seed House, bought the estate and converted the old residence into apartments.

Two Barber homes still stand on the east side of the CNR tracks at 121 and 127 Mountainview Road North. Another earlier Barber residence at 35 Park Street is known as 'Willow Bank'.

A brief outline of some of John R's positions throughout his industrious life illustrates his great importance on a national level and in the community. After his father's death in 1880 he became sole proprietor of the paper mill holdings; he was president and manager of Toronto Paper Manufacturing company, Toronto and Cornwall; founder and president of Barber-Ellis; president of Nipigon Pump and Paper Co.; Leadville Mining Co.; Canadian Brass and Tube Works, Toronto; and Floral View Greenhouses Co., Georgetown. He served as a director of the Anglo-American Fire Insurance Co. and Dominion Consolidated Mines.

John R. also served as a member of the Georgetown High School Board and was president of the Mechanics Institute, Reeve of Georgetown 1865-1875, Warden of Halton County 1878 and represented Halton at the

BERWICK HALL, JOHN R. BARBER'S HOME AT 139 MAIN STREET SOUTH, WAS DESIGNED BY PROMINENT TORONTO ARCHITECT EDWARD LENNOX.

Ontario Legislature as a Liberal, from 1898 to 1905.

Although a Liberal most of his life, John R. cast a vote for the Conservatives in 1916. Being a military man he differed with the Liberal stand on conscription.

John R. sold his interests in the paper business in 1911. The old paper mill on the Credit and the coated paper mill which he had constructed in 1905 were sold to the Provincial Paper Company. The old mill was partially utilized by Delta Craft furniture and the coated paper mill near the railway station was operated by Abitibi Paper until 1991.

Colonel John R. Barber Jr., was born in Berwick Hall in 1904 and was the only son of John R. and his second wife. He attended public and high schools in Georgetown and graduated from the University of Toronto in 1927. From 1928 to 1931 he was stage manager for Hart House at the University of Toronto. Colonel Barber was later elected a member of the Toronto Stock Exchange and by 1934 formed a brokerage in Toronto with a Mr. Amos. The partnership was dissolved in 1938.

Like his father, John R. Jr. was a military man. He was active with the 20th Halton Rifles (now the Lorne Scots) from 1925. In 1941 the regiment was called to Hamilton for training before sailing for England and World War Two. While overseas John R. Barber was promoted from major to lieutenant-colonel, and then to full colonel. From 1957 he served as honorary colonel of the Lorne Scots.

Returning to civil life in Georgetown, John R. purchased the insurance and travel business of Elmer Thompson, Mill Street, in 1950 and also the Freeman Kersey insurance agency. The Thompson agency had opened in 1925, because many local businessmen did not have a full-time exclusive insurance agent to deal

JOHN R. BARBER (CENTRE) POSES WITH MEMBERS OF THE GEORGETOWN BOWLING CLUB IN 1907. A NUMBER OF PROMINENT AREA BUSINESSMEN APPEAR. TOP ROW (L-R) H. MCKAY, DR. NICKELL, G. GRAHAM, R. J. CREELMAN, F. M. SCARF, J. W. KENNEDY, DR. ELLIOT, F. J. BARBER, DR. WEBSTER. CENTRE ROW (L-R) A. D. THOMSON, E. FINLAY, REV. R. F. CAMERON, J. MCDERMID, J. R. BARBER, L. GRANT, H. W. KENNEDY, W. A. F. CAMPBELL. FRONT ROW (L-R) J. MCBEAN, R. R. BARBER, — BROOKS, A. H. COFFEN, H. BELL, A. E. HUSTISS

with. Previously some merchants sold insurance 'on the side'.

In 1960 Murray Henley entered into partnership with John R. in the travel and insurance business. Barber and Henley was sold in 1989 to Caledon Insurance and eventually was relocated to Brampton. John R. Barber died on September 26, 1991.

The other Barber businesses in Georgetown in more recent years were owned by three brothers, Keith, Robert, and Paul, sons of Charles H. Barber. Charles was the second son of John R. Sr. and managed the paper business in Cornwall. This branch of the family returned to Georgetown during the 1930's and operated the Georgetown Floral Company on King Street.

Keith Barber's former home at the corner of King and Union Streets (46 King Street) was the office of the floral company and the former antique shop at the rear was once a boiler room for the greenhouses. Paul and Robert Barber started a sign business in approximately 1947 upstairs in the H.T. Arnold building (at Guelph and Mill Streets), but eventually Paul separated and owned the Barber Piano and Organ company and Barber's Jewellers on Main Street.

The paper mills and dynamo ruins remain as monuments to the Barbers' tremendous energy and ingenuity. William, Joseph and James Streets are named after the remarkable Irish emigrants who were part of the family that played an important part in the history of Georgetown as well as in paper making and hydro-electric power in Canada. ∞

DAYFOOT FAMILY: EARLY CANADIAN BOOTMAKERS

The Dayfoots brought national recognition to Georgetown with their popular work boots. They can be regarded as pioneers in the leather and shoe trade in Canada.

It was 1838 that J. B. Dayfoot and his brother P. W. Dayfoot arrived in Upper Canada from Vermont. They did not come directly to Georgetown but established a tannery in Hamilton.

J.B. Dayfoot and Co. came to Georgetown in 1843 and the tannery was near the corner of Mill and John Streets. A small dam was built just south of the Canadian National Railway tunnel where Silver Creek wanders through, and resultant water power drove machinery in the tannery. Gradually the tanning business branched out into shoemaking. The tannery burned in 1868 and was never re-built.

The firm known as J. B. Dayfoot & Co. was formed in 1892 after the death of John B. Dayfoot, for whom John Street was named. The firm specialized in manufacturing a heavy work boot which was sold to farmers, prospectors, lumberjacks and miners. The Dayfoot label was a popular one in shoe stores throughout Ontario and all the Western provinces. 'Solid Clear Through' was the company's advertising slogan and a high regard for quality was always maintained.

The shoe factory employed at various times 50 to 100 local people, while a small sales force visited lumber camps and mining towns promoting the Dayfoot line. Skilled machine operators were always in demand as a quantity of intricate machinery was required to carry on successfully.

The shoe factory reflects the modernization program a successful early industrialist had to introduce. The factory was eventually hydro-electrically powered. This system replaced a gasoline engine, which replaced a steam system, which in turn replaced the water turbine power used in the old tannery.

Dayfoot's was a family business in every respect. After the death of the two founding brothers, J.B. and P. W. Dayfoot, the new generation utilized various talents in keeping the company active. Charles acted as president, Harry as sales manager, Warner as factory foreman, Philo worked in the factory, while sister Gertrude was bookkeeper and office manager.

The Dayfoots were always very community-minded. Michael Dayfoot, father of J. B., was chosen to be first Deacon of the Georgetown Baptist Church at its inau-

CHARLES B. DAYFOOT, 1916.

gural meeting held on October 16, 1847 at a home in the village. The 'village' at this time contained about a dozen dwellings, whose occupants were either employed at the Barber Brothers' mills or Dayfoot's tannery. Michael was the first to carry the name Dayfoot after its change from 'Dafoe' at the time of the American Revolution. In 1866, when a group of Baptists decided to erect the church building which stands at 14 Main Street South, two of the principal contributors to the $8 000 project were J. B. and George Dayfoot. Harry Dayfoot was Georgetown Hydro commissioner for a number of years during the 1930's.

J. B. Dayfoot and Co. was sold in 1944 to Ed Johnston who later bought out the Gravlin-Bale Company in Campbellford, Ontario and consolidated the two businesses there. The shoe factory was then sold in 1947 to the Hedley Shoe Company in Toronto, who operated under the name Georgetown Shoe Company for a number of years.

The shoe factory sat idle, then was used as a warehouse and sales outlet for a boat company before being converted into apartments by Albert Euteneier in 1966.

The only remnant of the family name in Georgetown is a result of Victoria Drive being renamed Dayfoot Drive on January 1, 1974. ∞

THE DAYFOOT FAMILY (L-R) PHILO (FACTORY WORKER), WARNER (FOREMAN), GERTRUDE (OFFICE MANAGER), CHARLES (PRESIDENT) AND HARRY (SALES MANAGER).

THE DAYFOOT SHOE COMPANY DOMINATES THIS VIEW OF GEORGETOWN FROM THE RAILROAD STATION AREA.

THE OLD PONDS OF GEORGETOWN

The earliest industries in this area relied on water: no water, no mills. Rivers were dammed to form ponds and mill races cut to turn the machinery for the first saw and grist mills and tanneries.

When George Kennedy arrived here in 1823 it was the available water supply along Silver Creek which attracted him and resulted in the establishment of a saw mill.

The Barber brothers travelled along the northern shore of Lake Ontario and ventured up the Credit River to seek an advantageous site for a mill. When they purchased land from Kennedy in 1837 they also bought the rights for damming the river. This purchase resulted in the area's first industrial boom.

There were three major ponds within the incorporated village of Georgetown. One, on Silver Creek on each side of the Grand Trunk line (near the John Street culvert) generated power for the Dayfoot Tannery.

Further south along Silver Creek was the pond that provided water power for operating the Barbers' woollen mill as early as 1837 and later for a foundry which provided steel used for constructing the Grand Trunk railway during the early 1850's.

The site of this pond, bounded by Guelph, Mill and Park Streets, was the first industrial hub of the village. Harley-Kay Knitting Machine Co., Lawson's Lumber Mill (later Georgetown Lumber then Beaver Lumber), Reynold's Paint factory, Arnold's Glove Works (now Carpet Barn) are just a few of the industries once located in the area. It is little wonder that Park Street, which leads into the district, was once called Factory Street. The concrete sluice gate which formed a part of the dam can still be found at the foot of the Park Street hill. The Silver Creek Apartments are now near this location.

This pond was known as Wilber Lake and village folk enjoyed many afternoons canoeing there. Picnics were also held along its banks. It is generally believed the name 'Wilber' was derived from combining the family names Williams (of Glen Williams) and Barber (the enterprising Irish brothers). There were probably periods when the pond dried up, as it was also dubbed 'Lake Sometime'… "sometimes it was there and sometimes it wasn't"! Wilber Lake disappeared during the construction of a wooden trestle about 1915 for the Toronto Suburban Railway, and Silver Creek is now a mere trickle compared with earlier years.

Charles Young in his reminiscence of old Georgetown relates that "before dams were built to impede their

WILBER PARK LAKE TAKEN FROM NEAR ST. GEORGE'S ANGLICAN CHURCH. MAIN STREET BUILDINGS ARE SEEN AT THE TOP OF THE PHOTO.

passage, sea salmon swarmed up the Credit and all streams falling into lake Ontario, and that in the spawning season they were packed so thick in the Credit that if they had not moved one could have walked on their backs dry-shod".

The Lawson Pond was on the site of the present Sid-Mac Building at 32 Main Street South. This pond supplied water by flume to Water Street (now Mill) to operate a flour mill and it, too, was drained for the coming of the radial line.

The vanished ponds which once graced Georgetown helped generate power for the earliest industries, which in turn contributed to the growth of the village. Later they were a source of recreation after the advent of hydro-electric power. ◈

ST. GEORGE'S ANGLICAN CHURCH OVERLOOKS WILBER LAKE.

LAWSON'S TROUT POND. SIX LADIES POSE IN 1909.

GEORGETOWN AGRICULTURAL SOCIETY

Agriculture was the most important aspect of the settler's life and agricultural societies played a major role in the community. In the early days it was not unusual to see farmers from miles around herd their finest livestock on the roadside leading to the annual agricultural fair.

HORSE AND BUGGY AT GEORGETOWN DRIVING PARK.

The Georgetown Agricultural Society, one of the oldest in the province, was founded in 1846 and was originally known as The Esquesing Agricultural Society. The first meeting and actual fair were held that same year in Stewarttown when the area was still a dense forest with some land cleared by the earliest settlers.

Pioneer families brought their produce and livestock, including oxen, to Stewarttown for the annual fair. Vegetables, grains, fruit and ladies' crafts were displayed in Stewarttown Hall. Outdoor exhibits and livestock shows were held (behind the old Stewarttown Schoolhouse) on top of the hill to the south of the settlement.

About 1875 the fall fair was moved from Stewarttown to Georgetown and held at the market square (near Market and Park Avenue). A 2.5-metre high wooden fence was built around the fair site. An old military drill shed, near the present library site on Church Street, housed the indoor displays.

The annual fall fair has always been one of the most significant events in agricultural-based towns like Georgetown. Since its earliest times the fair has always attracted several hundred — and later thousands — to the town. The fair was not only a social highlight of the year, but also one of the most significant business days for shops, restaurants and hotels.

The fair moved to Georgetown Park in 1889. Recognizing that the Esquesing Agricultural Society was truly a township organisation, the fall fair alternated between Acton and Georgetown until 1908. Georgetown then became home for the fall fair. (Acton had organized its own agricultural society.) The name was eventually changed from Esquesing to The Georgetown Agricultural Society in 1966 to avoid any confusion about the location of the fall fair. When the fair moved from Market Street to Georgetown Park the armoury building was made available for indoor exhibits.

The early fairs were truly agricultural shows featuring the finest livestock and produce from area farmers. Oxen, imported shorthorns, show and work horses, Berkshire pigs, poultry and Leicester sheep were among the exhibits. In 1907 the Society held its first plowing match on William Cleave's farm which was immediately north of the fairgrounds. Road and carriage horses were the pride of the early fairs. Harness racing was eliminated in the late 1950's after a horse-hitch broke loose during a race and officials recognized the potential for a serious accident.

Although there was no midway in the earliest fairs, games of chance, taffy apples, popcorn and candy were always available. Cy Kennedy, from Georgetown, would travel the local fall fair circuit in the early 1900's with a team of horses and a wagon filled with sweets for children.

In 1944 the Halton Crop Improvement Association was experimenting to determine if husking corn could be a viable crop in Halton. A competition was held in conjunction with the Agricultural Society with 13 entries. A summer drive through the north Halton farming area will confirm that the results were successful.

School exhibits have played an important part of the Fall Fair since the early 1940's. A typical school prize list in those days included competitions for penmanship, illustrations of nursery rhymes, paper construction, painting on glass and essays about farm life. Prizes in 1949 were 50¢, 25¢ and 15¢ for first, second and third place.

Garfield McGilvray has been associated with the Agricultural Society since the early 1930's. He first attended Society meetings as a reporter for *The Georgetown Herald* when they were held upstairs at The McGibbon Hotel. After the crash of 1929 the Society was experiencing a very difficult time, and McGilvray and Craig Reid, who farmed on the Ninth Concession to the east of town, were approached about forming a nucleus to get the fair back on track. Mr. McGilvray served as president for four years and 15 years as secretary. Along with his wife, Emmaline, they have missed only one fair day in over 50 years.

THE GEORGETOWN CREAMERY TRUCK OWNED BY MORRIS SAXE WON FIRST PRIZE FOR 'BEST DECORATED' AT THE FALL FAIR IN THE 1920'S. DRIVER WAS JIMMY WOODS.

In 1936 the first baby contest was held at the fair. Nathaniel Guthrie, a local boy who went on to become Deputy Chief of the Toronto Police Department, organized and sponsored the contest. Guthrie enjoyed returning to Georgetown to the annual fair and provided the prizes which included silver baby mugs, silver dollars and Government Savings Certificates. By 1947 there were almost 50 entries and the contest was sponsored by Robertson's Department Store from Hamilton. In 1954 the baby show was abandoned due to recurring inclement weather, the lack of a warm dry building and the amount of equipment and volunteers required made the baby contest out of proportion for an agricultural show.

The Agricultural Society celebrated its centenary in 1946. The Ontario Department of Agriculture provided a $1 000 grant for the erection of a pylon and flagpole. The pylon was built by local stone masons Logan and Haines. T. L. Kennedy, Ontario Minister of Agriculture, was represented at the dedication. A ladies' section of the Agricultural Society was formed during its centennial year.

During the 1940's and 50's dances, euchres, dinners and cooking classes were held at various locations including the Rose Room (at Georgetown Memorial Arena) and community halls in Stewarttown, Limehouse and Norval to help raise funds. Tory Gregg, a popular Wingham radio announcer, and later Vince Mountford, an accomplished emcee from Brampton, acted as masters of ceremony at the fall fair for many years.

In 1952 a new horse barn was erected with volunteer labour and equipment. The building, however, has been used mainly as an exhibition hall. The fall fair featured a heritage costume contest and mammoth parade to the fair grounds in 1967 during Canada's Centennial year. The town-owned wooden grandstand was completely destroyed by fire in 1968. Although the fair has never missed a year during the two world wars and the depression, one Saturday in 1977 was completely 'washed-out' due to continuous rainfall.

In the very early years the fair was a one-day event. It eventually expanded to two days and in 1982 the Society held the first three-day fair when Sunday was included. The Georgetown Fall Fair now regularly records attendance figures exceeding 18 000. ◈

JOHN A. WILLOUGHBY AND THE UNION BUS

Beginning with small land transactions in 1907, J. A. Willoughby's firm became the largest rural real estate company in Canada during the thirties. The original realty office was on Mill Street in the livery building which now houses The Royal Canadian Legion.

It was 1901 when John A. Willoughby, at the age of 25, established himself in the business world. His first venture was the purchase of a livery stable and bus business from H. A. McCallum in Georgetown.

The 'bus' was a coach which carried passengers between the railroad station and the downtown area. The Union bus, as it was known, was a success. This success can be attributed not only to the fact that Georgetown was a very enterprising village in the early 1900's, but also because the train was the main mode of transportation and Georgetown was the junction of the Grand Trunk and Hamilton & North West Railways.

The livery stable, reported in Toronto newspapers to be one of the finest in Ontario, was located at 127 Mill Street. This stone building was erected in 1906 and could hold up to 30 horses.

The livery business operated on a 24-hour basis and so a bedroom was maintained upstairs for the 'night' man. An early description of the livery stable from a Toronto newspaper indicates that a paint room existed where "Mr. Willoughby keeps his vehicles freshly painted at short intervals."

Willoughby's business concerns were not confined to the livery establishment. John A. was instrumental in promoting the establishment of the Georgetown Coated Paper Mills which came into existence in 1910 and through time was purchased by Domtar. He was the first President of the company which eventually closed its doors in 1977.

In 1904 Mr. Willoughby was elected to municipal council and served as Reeve of Georgetown from 1905 to 1908. While a member of the Board of Education and Library Board, Willoughby gave a parcel of land for the site of a new library, but in the meantime the Congregational church on Church Street was donated for the library in 1912. The parcel of land donated by John A. was then sold for $500 to J. B. Mackenzie and

WILLOUGHBY'S UNION BUS AT THE GEORGETOWN GRAND TRUNK STATION.

'THE GOLF LINKS' DEVELOPED BY JOHN A. WILLOUGHBY DURING THE 1920'S IS NOW NORTH HALTON GOLF & COUNTRY CLUB ON MAPLE AVENUE. THE WILLOUGHBY HOME APPEARS ON THE LEFT.

the money used to purchase equipment for the library.

Willoughby was commissioned as a real estate agent to purchase the right-of-way for the Toronto Suburban Railway Company for the portion of the line between Georgetown and Guelph.

Willoughby built his business on honesty and integrity. John A's son, Bertram once headed Gibson-Willoughby Real Estate which is now part of Royal LePage.

Due to the firm's early emphasis on farm transactions, Bertram studied field husbandry at the Ontario Agricultural College to be better able to relate with farmers and talk their own language. Two real estate firms, Gibson Brothers and J. A. Willoughby, merged in 1966 and were bought out by Bertram Willoughby in 1971.

The former Willoughby residence was located on a 60-hectare farm to the west of Georgetown on Maple Avenue. During the 1920's John A. created a nine-hole golf course on the property. A group of local businessmen bought the estate and developed it into what is now the North Halton Golf and Country Club. ∞

J. A. WILLOUGHBY, PRESIDENT OF THE GEORGETOWN 'VICTORIAS' ABOUT 1915. IN THE PHOTOGRAPH ARE : TOP ROW (L-R) E. JONES, H. ORMEROD, S. DEWHURST, J. MAKIN, J. SCOTT, J. AYRES. CENTRE ROW (L-R) J. CARTER, REV. A. B. HIGGINSON, J. BLAIR, J. A. WILLOUGHBY, J. WILLIAMS. FRONT ROW (L-R) W. BLAIR, A. HERBERT (CAPT.), F. COLLIER.

H.P. LAWSON: PROVIDER OF GEORGETOWN'S FIRST HYDRO POWER

Electric light power from H. P. Lawson's mill in 'The Glen' was only available until mid-evening to Georgetown residents but if you were having a gathering at home the power time could be extended for a small fee. The Lawson mill in Glen Williams was the first hydro source for Georgetown.

Researchers of the early history of any community in southern Ontario inevitably find that a tannery, grist mill or saw mill was one of the first industrial undertakings and probably formed the basis of what is now the present town or village.

The Halton region is certainly no exception to this basic premise, as mills of this type thrived especially during the late 1800's. This was certainly true of the saw mills in Esquesing Township where a tremendous amount of pine was available.

The earliest entrepreneur in the local lumber business was Henry Pratt Lawson, better know as H.P. He was born in Fifeshire, Scotland in 1840 and came to Canada in 1852, settling with his family near Stewarttown.

H.P. Lawson was one of the most enterprising men of his time in the Georgetown-Acton area. He became an extensive landholder in Esquesing and subsequently had a number of sawmills and lumbering operations under his control.

It was H.P. Lawson's power plant in Glen Williams that provided Georgetown with its first hydro-electric power. Many people mistakenly attribute the first such power to be from the Barber Brothers' dynamo which was used only for their industrial paper mill site on the Credit.

From the Lawson mill located in the Glen and purchased from Joseph Williams, the power was generated from a dynamo which used the energy of the Credit from a dam in Glen Williams. The power plant was later converted to a steam boiler to generate power because silt accumulated at the dam and reduced water pressure.

The power was then transmitted to Georgetown from what is now part of The Williams Mill Creative Arts School. Some sources relate the line ran along Confederation Street, Glen Williams and Mountainview Road into town, while others state that the transmission wires ran across the McMaster farm and up and over the fields and hills through the former Smith and Stone site into the town transformers. The transformers were located at the old Town Hall overlooking the downtown from Cross and Back Streets.

A daughter of H. P.'s, Mrs. Arnott Early, could remember Sir Adam Beck coming to her father's home for dinner and to negotiate a deal for the Ontario Hydro takeover of the power company. Beck, a former Mayor of London, Ontario and member of the Ontario Legislature was instrumental in the formation of Ontario Hydro.

The most central sawmill owned by H. P. Lawson was near the former Georgetown Hydro building on

HENRY PRATT LAWSON (1840-1920).

AT THE CORNER OF MILL AND BACK STREETS, THE H. P. LAWSON SAWMILL WAS A FAMILIAR PART OF OLD GEORGETOWN. A TEAM OF OXEN ARE IN THE FOREGROUND WHILE THE MCGIBBON HOTEL AND MAIN STREET BUILDINGS CAN BE SEEN AT THE TOP OF THIS 1909 PHOTO.

LAWSON'S TROUT POND WAS SITUATED WHERE 32 MAIN STREET SOUTH NOW STANDS.

Mill Street. It derived its power from Silver Creek, which ran through the property, and was later converted to steam power. This mill was eventually taken over by the Kentner family. Beaver Lumber was the last company to operate a lumber business on the site. The fire that destroyed Beaver Lumber in the early 1970's marked the end of this industrial hub that had existed since the town's earliest days.

Lawson started a planing business in conjunction with his sawmills in 1897. J. B. Mackenzie bought this portion of Lawson's business interest on James Street in 1909. The Mackenzies operated a lumber business there until 1992.

It was in 1901 at the age of 61, that Lawson married Margaret Mabel Grant, the daughter of Major Lachlan Grant of Georgetown. They raised four children who became well-respected citizens of the area and later relocated. On April 19, 1922, a dedication service was held at Knox Presbyterian Church for the carillon of eight bells in memory of H. P. Lawson, who died on March 5, 1920.

The Lawson family was very active in community affairs. H. P. served on Esquesing Council and was Deputy-Reeve in 1893. Mrs. Lawson was an active member of the church and taught Sunday School classes for over 12 years. She died December 7, 1926 at the age of 51 and a plaque hangs in the church to her memory.

The Lawson home still stands at 11 Church Street, directly across from the Halton Hills Cultural Centre. In 1890 H. P. built the row of homes directly behind his at 51, 53, and 55 Market Street. These were for the 'better class' of the time and stand as monuments to a man who was reputed to have financially assisted many local merchants and manufacturers and was always willing to give a fellow citizen a helping hand when buying or erecting a home. ⚘

H.T. ARNOLD GLOVE WORKS

H. *T. Arnold advertised in the* Toronto Globe *and* The Star *to attract potential employees to relocate to Georgetown. He owned 16 houses in town and offered these to employees at very reasonable rents. Large families were encouraged to come because the father and older children would be able to work in his plant.*

Herbert Thomas Arnold, born March 14, 1858 was 18 when he left Yeovil, England, with his family. They settled at Johnston, New York. The Arnold family had been glove cutters for many years in the 'old country'. In 1878 Arnold left Johnston for Glen Williams to work for a Mr. Borad, a glove manufacturer.

In 1890 at the age of 32, Herbert decided to start a glove company of his own in Acton. He also operated a tannery during the 1890's at Glen Lawson, a small industrial centre near Dolly Varden, about 2.5 kilometres south-east of Acton along the Grand Trunk Railway line.

The business in Acton prospered and by 1901 Arnold had expanded to Georgetown. The new factory, at the corner of Guelph and Mill Streets, was a three-storey

brick building measuring 37 x 12 metres. It was reputed to be one of the largest and best equipped glove factories in the area. Hydro-electric power was used to operate the Singer sewing machines and an auxiliary gasoline engine, built by Thomas Speight of Georgetown, was maintained to prevent a delay in production in the event of a power failure.

In 1912 the H. T. Arnold Glove Company employed about 110 people and had six travelling sales representatives on the road. The firm manufactured a high quality line of fine gloves for men and women and a coarse work glove. Sheepskin, pigskin, calfskin, and buckskin were the leathers mainly imported from England and the United States. Over 200 varieties of gloves were made in the plant at the rate of 100 pairs per day.

In 1915 the firm purchased the W. H. Storey Glove Works in Acton and ceased their operations in the Georgetown plant at Guelph and Mill Streets in 1922.

Ken McMillan operated a farm implement agency in the same Georgetown building, and more recently Canadian Tire and Mel's Antiques were situated there. It has also housed Goodyear Tire and currently the Carpet Barn is at 26 Guelph Street.

In 1880, Arnold married Mary Graham at Glen Williams and after her death in 1901 he married Melvina Bennett in 1905. Melvina was the daughter of a Georgetown dentist who had his practice over the Creelman factory office on Main Street (near Young's Pharmacy 45 and 47 Main Street South). The Arnolds had nine children (six boys and three girls) and most took an interest in the family business.

H. T. Arnold lived in a frame house at the corner of Main and Kennedy Streets from 1901 until he purchased the Goodwillie estate at 52 Queen Street in 1906. The large brick house, with a mansard roof, was erected in 1880 for the magnificent sum of $6 000. Mr. Goodwillie

H. T. ARNOLD AND MARY GRAHAM WERE MARRIED AT GLEN WILLIAMS IN 1880.

GRANDVIEW HOUSE, THE ARNOLD RESIDENCE FROM 1906 TO 1932, 52 QUEEN STREET.

SALES REPRESENTATIVES' CARS PARKED BESIDE THE H. T. ARNOLD GLOVE FACTORY AT THE CORNER OF GUELPH AND MILL STREETS. THE TORONTO SUBURBAN 'RADIAL' TRESTLE IS VISIBLE ON THE RIGHT.

was a solicitor who began his practice in Georgetown in 1876. The mansion, named Grandview House, had 28 rooms and the grounds included tennis courts and bowling greens. Two people were employed full-time to maintain the lawns and housekeep.

The Arnold family resided there from 1906 until 1932 when H. T. moved to Toronto. The house was sold in 1937 to J. B. Mackenzie and was converted to an apartment building.

H.T. Arnold died January 2, 1937 in his 79th year after being struck by a cyclist in Toronto while waiting for the bus to Acton.

William Arnold, the eldest son, became president of the firm in 1937 and occupied this position until his death in 1945. The third son, Roy, took control of the business in 1945 until the company dissolved in 1954.

Many descendants of H. T. Arnold remain in the community in which he played an important role. ∞

TIMOTHY EATON: EARLY DAYS WITH THE REIDS IN NORTH HALTON

In 1854 at 21 years of age Timothy Eaton set sail for Canada from his native Ireland and made the Georgetown area his first home. Most of his brothers and sisters had already emigrated to Canada and had started out on the Robert Reid farm on the Ninth Concession east of Georgetown. (Reid had married Timothy's sister, Margaret.) One of Eaton's first positions in Canada was as bookkeeper-clerk at a small general store in Glen Williams.

Robert Reid (1815-1896) emigrated from Ireland in the late 1830's and eventually settled in the Peel-Halton area and worked for Timothy Street, a surveyor and local industrialist after whom Streetsville is named. Street owed Reid back wages and in lieu of payment he deeded the north-east half of Lot 15, Ninth Line in Esquesing Township to Reid on December 9, 1840. A price was established for the 40 hectares and Reid paid the difference which amounted to 37 pounds, 5 shillings and 8 pence.

Robert Reid married Mary Bowman Fraser, who died in 1851 four days after giving birth to a son. The Reid family were related to an Irish family named Eaton from Clogher County in Antrim and in the same year Margaret Eaton (1824-1900) said goodbye to Ireland and arrived in Georgetown to marry Reid, her first cousin. The newlyweds left on a touring honeymoon in an elegant new carriage with brass lamps. Robert built a brick house on the farm prior to Margaret's arrival and this house—which was situated near the present Centennial School on Delrex Boulevard—became a rendezvous for other Eaton immigrants.

Timothy Eaton (1834-1907), Margaret's youngest brother, arrived at the Reid farm in 1854. He worked for his brother-in-law for a short time and was soon employed as a bookkeeper-clerk at a general store located at 523 Main Street in Glen Williams and would sometimes sleep under the counter overnight rather than walk down the Ninth Line to the Reid farm.

Charles Young in his reminiscences of old Georgetown relates that Timothy Eaton and his brother James were employed by Charles' father James for a few years. James Young, one of the founders of the village of Georgetown, settled here in 1843 and operated one of the area's first grocery stores at the corner of Main and Mill Streets on the site of the Canadian Imperial Bank of Commerce, 82 Main Street South.

In approximately 1856 Timothy and brother James moved from Georgetown to Kirkton, Ontario and opened a general store and post office. They later amalgamated with another brother, Robert, at St. Mary's, Ontario. Timothy set up the T. Eaton Bakery there and met his wife, Margaret Wilson Beattie (1841-1933). In 1869 he relocated to Toronto with his young family and purchased a dry goods store from William Jennings at 178 Yonge Street. Here he implemented his 'one fair price for all' and 'goods satisfactory or money refunded' policies. On August 22, 1883 Eaton opened Toronto's first department store at 190 Yonge Street.

After Timothy Eaton had laid a solid business foundation in Toronto, he purchased property immediately south of Georgetown and shipped fresh milk and apples to his employees' cafeterias and restaurants. It was an Eaton who drove one of the first cars into Georgetown up the Norval Hill causing a great commotion! Timothy Eaton's sister, Sarah, is buried at Greenwood Cemetery in Georgetown.

Timothy Eaton Reid (1861-1922), eldest son of Robert Reid and Margaret Eaton, eventually took over the original farm purchased by his father from Timothy Street in 1840. Two further generations of Reids operated this same farm—Robert and his son W. T. Craig Reid. There was a three-year period (1923-1926) when Harold Lyons of Norval, owned the property. Robert Reid purchased the farm in 1926 and it was once

TIMOTHY EATON AT ST. MARY'S, ONTARIO IN 1865.

TIMOTHY EATON WORKED AT THIS STORE IN GLEN WILLIAMS SITUATED AT 523 MAIN STREET.

again in the Reid name until purchased by Rex Heslop Developments in 1955. The following year the brick home built in 1851 by Robert Reid for his bride was demolished to make way for the subdivision. In 1956 Craig Reid moved to a new home on Chipper Court. A farm which he purchased in 1964 on Ten Sideroad, immediately south of town, was the host farm for the International Plowing match held in September, 1974.

Another Reid farm which sat immediately north on Lot 16, Ninth Line (Mountainview Road) was purchased by Robert Reid on November 28, 1865 from John White. Robert Fraser Reid, the only child of Robert Reid and Margaret Fraser, took over the farm July 11, 1876 and built the brick farm house in 1886 which now sits at 75 McIntyre Crescent with the original slate roof. He also built a new barn in 1890 which had one of the first silos in the district. This farm was taken over by the third son of Robert Fraser Reid, William

Henry, on April 1, 1913 and later by his son Henry Craig who sold to Rex Heslop in 1955.

The Reid family have farmed in this community since 1840 and for over a century most of the land in the present eastern limits of Georgetown was held by the Reid family.

William John Reid, the youngest child of Robert Reid and Margaret Eaton, once owned a farm at the corner of Armstrong Ave. and Highway 7. In April 1867 Robert Reid purchased a property which he sold to his son James Henry Reid in 1888. This same property is now the location of Zellers and A & P Food Store.

The Reid family, dedicated Presbyterians, helped establish the Union and Norval Presbyterian Churches. The family is still active in the Norval church.

The brick farm house at 75 McIntyre Crescent and Reid Court are reminders of the contribution to the development of this community by the Reids for over 150 years. ⬦

CREAMERY BUTTER
REID'S
THE T. EATON CO. LIMITED
190 YONGE ST.   TORONTO, CAN.

A LABEL FROM REID'S GEORGETOWN FARM FOR BUTTER SOLD IN EATON'S YONGE STREET STORE IN TORONTO.

THE ROBERT FRASER REID FAMILY POSE AT SHERMAN & KAY STUDIOS IN GEORGETOWN. (FRONT) WEIR, FRASER, JOSEPHINE. (SEATED CENTRE) ROBERT FRASER, JAMES, AGNES. (BACK) WILLIAM, ROBERT.

ROBERT REID (1815-1896).

CLEAVE FAMILY AND THE EARLY MORNING MILK

Need some milk in a hurry? Way back it was unlawful for unpasteurized milk to be sold, but local residents can remember climbing 'back' fences to buy a bucket of milk at the Cleave farm.

Richard and Grace Cleave and their six children left Devon, England, for Canada in the mid-1850's. Mrs. Cleave was pregnant as she endured the tedious voyage and gave birth to their seventh child, William, shortly after their arrival.

The family made their first home in the Dundas, Ontario area, eventually farming in Eramosa Township, near Rockwood. It was from this home that the eldest son, John, is said to have walked to Hamilton with only a pack on his back and a rifle for protection. Upon arriving he secured a position driving a 'team' at the steel mills where he remained most of his life.

The Cleave family came to Georgetown in 1878. Two brothers, William and James, married two Walker sisters, Agnes and Charlotte, who were descendants of George Kennedy, the founder of Georgetown. William (1848-1923) purchased 80 hectares in 1907 between the Seventh and Eighth Lines (now Trafalgar Road and Main Street) south of the Grand Trunk Line.

Within three or four years the Cleaves bricked the original clapboard house and established a good milk business. One of William's sons, Percy, recalled selling milk to the Bennett Hotel which sat directly across Main Street from the McGibbon Hotel at 78 Main Street South. Chores started early on the Cleave farm as milk had to be delivered before 7:30 for guests at the hotel: refrigerators hadn't been invented and milk couldn't be stored overnight at this fine hotel! The Cleaves peddled milk throughout the village in a large milk can and a ladle was used to fill pitchers brought out by each family for their daily supply.

Brothers Percy and Harold Cleave took over the farm on their father's death in 1923. They continued the dairy business but when a pasteurisation law was introuced the milk was then sold in bulk to Toronto dairies.

Although the Cleave farm was subdivided into building lots by 1953, Harold Cleave continued to reside in the old farm house which still stands at 5 Cleaveholm

THE CHILDREN OF RICHARD AND GRACE CLEAVE, WHO CAME TO CANADA IN THE 1850'S, POSE FOR A STUDIO 'LIKENESS' IN GEORGETOWN. BACK ROW (L-R) WILLIAM, JAMES, EDWIN AND JOHN. FRONT ROW (L-R) GRACE, ANN AND SUSAN.

Drive. The Georgetown Hospital, Park School, The Christian Reform Church School, the wartime houses on Churchill Crescent and the Marywood Meadows subdivisions are on the farm purchased by the Cleaves in 1907.

In the early 1920's when the gravity-fed water supply at Silver Creek was deemed to be inadequate, a portion of marshy land was purchased from the Cleave property and a pumping station established. The Toronto Suburban Radial line ran through this part of the farm and Princess Anne Drive now follows its former right-of-way.

The raising of dairy cattle ended at the Cleave farm in 1950 when the barn was completely ruined by fire. Beef cattle, however, were grazed later on the Cleaves 'upper' farm, known as Wildwood Manor and now part of The Watchtower Bible & Tract Society property. Relatives and neighbours would congregate at the old milk house each Sunday morning at the 'upper' farm for some talk and 'refreshment'. This weekly assemblage became a ritual and was dubbed the 'farm forum'.

The Cleaves have always played a role in community organizations but probably the most prominent was Harold (1891-1974). He served a total of 19 years on the local council and was Reeve of Georgetown and Warden in 1935, and served as Mayor of Georgetown from 1944 to 1946 and again in 1950 and 1951. Harold was always a respected and hard-working individual who enjoyed his political service. He not only participated in sports during his youth, but acted as coach for many early hockey teams.

Another Cleave farm, on Lot 16, Concession 10, was purchased by James Cleave about 1884. This farm also produced milk which helped supply the village. Annie Clark's Ice Cream Parlour (once situated in a wooden frame building on Main Street South) received fresh milk from the farm. When payment for the milk 'came due' on a Saturday, many local children were treated by the Cleaves to some ice cream.

When James retired from the farm in 1924, his son Wilbert took over. In May, 1954 the farm was sold to Rex Heslop and it now makes up a portion of the industrial park which includes part of Armstrong Avenue and Todd Road. The frame farm house dating from 1892 was constructed of clear pine supplied by the old Kennedy Sawmill near Wildwood Road at a cost of $3 400. The house was relocated to 10 McIntyre Crescent

HARVEST TIME AT THE WILLIAM CLEAVE FARM (1908). HAROLD IS STANDING ON THE LOAD OF SHEAVES, PERCY IS AT THE DOOR WITH THE HORSES AND FATHER WILLIAM CLEAVE LOOKS ON IN THE CENTRE OF THE PHOTOGRAPH. THE BARN WAS COMPLETELY DESTROYED BY FIRE IN 1950. THE BRICK FARM HOUSE STILL STANDS AT 5 CLEAVEHOLM DRIVE.

THIS AERIAL PHOTOGRAPH TAKEN IN THE 1940'S SHOWS THE JAMES CLEAVE FARM WHICH HIS SON WILBERT EVENTUALLY TOOK OVER. GORDON ALCOTT MEMORIAL ARENA NOW STANDS ON THE SAME SITE AS THE HOUSE. THE HOUSE, BUILT IN 1892, WAS RELOCATED TO 10 MCINTYRE CRESCENT.

by Heslop and is now the residence and office of Dr. A. MacIntosh. The Gordon Alcott Memorial Arena on Guelph Street sits on the former site of the farmhouse.

George Cleave purchased a farm on the Ninth Line (Mountainview Road) immediately south of the 'hollow' of Silver Creek. He was a member of Esquesing Township council for 13 years, served as Reeve for two years and was Warden of Halton County in 1948. ∞

SHEPHERD FAMILY: MEMORIES OF THE UNDERGROUND RAILROAD

The first members of the Shepherd family in the Georgetown area had survived the hardships and dangers associated with the 'Underground Railroad'. A generation later, Henry Shepherd, well-known for his military stance was reputed to have been one of the finest soldiers to ever 'don the King's uniform'.

When United Empire Loyalists came from the United States to settle in Canada many officers and the wealthy brought with them their black slaves. By 1793, Lieutenant Governor John Graves Simcoe had introduced legislation to abolish slavery in Upper Canada but met with bitter opposition. This resentment came mainly from farmers who insisted slaves were needed to do farm work. The legislation was then changed to prohibit any further slaves from entering the province and provided that children of slaves were to be liberated upon reaching the age of 25.

Slavery was finally abolished in the Canadas in August 1833. This was approximately 30 years before the American slaves were freed.

American slaves made their way into Canada in great numbers. By 1840 Chatham, Ontario was one of the principal terminals of the 'Underground Railroad'. The Fugitive Slave Act, passed in September 1850, jeopardized free blacks and fugitives living in the Northern United States, so the immigration of blacks into Canada during the 1850's increased, as once on Canadian soil they could no longer be pursued. It was during this time a brave black mother and her son made their way into Canada and eventually located in the Stewarttown area. They are reputed to have been the first black settlers in the district.

The young boy was John Henry Shepherd, born in 1859. The Shepherd family had been inadvertently separated during their travels to the 'promised land' in Canada. The Shepherds made their home in a comfortable log cabin near the old grandstand at what is now Georgetown Fair Grounds. A pathway through this area was a short-cut between Georgetown and Stewarttown and was used by Mrs. Shepherd who kept house for Colonel John Murray on his farm near Stewarttown.

Colonel Murray headed the Stewarttown military unit and later served in the 20th Halton Rifles, known now as the Lorne Scots.

An agreement was made with the Murrays that young Johnny Shepherd would be raised at their homestead should anything happen to his mother. In a few years the mother died and was buried in the park near the old log cabin. The body was later moved to St. George's Anglican cemetery.

The Murrays fulfilled their agreement with Mrs. Shepherd and raised the young boy, who arrived on their doorstep with his modest belongings on the morning of his mother's death. The relationship was a long and friendly one. John worked on the Murray farm and in the home was treated as one of the family.

The Murrays eventually hired a young English girl, Sarah Hartley (1872-1941), who was bonded to work in their home. John Shepherd and Sarah's meeting eventually resulted in wedlock.

John and Sarah originally lived in a cabin on the Murray farm, located on the Fifteenth Sideroad just west of Stewarttown. The Shepherds later moved into the village of Stewarttown and lived directly across from the old school house which was once used by Briggs Upholstery. In 1920 the family moved to Georgetown.

John Shepherd would walk up the railway tracks daily from Stewarttown when he worked at Ed Fleck's Coated Paper Mill (later Domtar). John suffered from a back problem and always stood in an arched position with his long arms prominent.

The Shepherds raised six children: Violet, Henry, John, Flora, Johnetta, and Jessie. 'Old' John Shepherd died in his sleep on September 5, 1948, at the age of 89. Each of John and Sarah's offspring played their role in the community, none more so than Henry Thomas

JOHN HENRY SHEPHERD (1859-1948).

Shepherd, who was born August 8, 1895 at Stewarttown. Henry's first encounter with labour was on area farms and eventually he delivered mail between Stewarttown and Ashgrove. He drove Willoughby's 'Union bus', which delivered passengers to and from the Grand Trunk Station in Georgetown. Henry, along with his father and brother John, worked at Georgetown Coated Paper Mill. He was employed there for 49 years.

As well as serving as Chief of Georgetown's Volunteer Fire Brigade in the 1930's and acting as a parade marshal for many years, Henry was a distinguished military man. He enlisted with the Halton Volunteer Rifles in 1911 and went into action with the 58th Battalion in World War One. During overseas service he was twice wounded. Upon returning home he re-enlisted with the Halton Rifles militia and eventually held the rank of Regimental Sergeant Major and served with the Lorne Rifles. With the outbreak of World War Two, Henry joined up, was given the rank of Company Sergeant Major and served at Newmarket Training Centre and was later appointed Fire Marshal there.

HENRY THOMAS SHEPHERD RECEIVES HIS M.B.E. FROM LIEUTENANT-GOVERNOR ALBERT MATHEWS IN TORONTO, JUNE 17, 1945.

On August 15, 1923, Henry Shepherd married Susanne Maude Cox in Georgetown at St. George's Anglican Church. The Cox family had relocated to Georgetown from Toronto and were employed by the H. T. Arnold Glove Works. Henry and Maude Shepherd raised seven girls: Helen, Doris, June, Violet, Mabel, Lillian, and Jacqueline. An only son John, died on September 3, 1939 only four years of age.

Henry was a founding member of the Georgetown Branch of the Royal Canadian Legion. A meeting to organize the Legion was held in the Town Hall on March 14, 1928 with three Guelph Legion members present. Henry was an active member throughout his military career but declined nominations to the Legion Executive. Much of his time was certainly spent at the Legion as more than once Mrs. Shepherd threatened to "send his bed down to the Legion Hall!" Henry was on the King's Honour List and was appointed a Member of the Order of the British Empire (M.B.E.). He was later presented with the first Certificate of Merit awarded by the local Legion.

Henry's brother John (1896-1970) was well known as a member of the Georgetown Citizens' Band. Apparently Henry made his debut with the tuba at home with intentions of joining the group... but his musical career came to an abrupt end when members of the family complained of the 'flat' sounds.

Henry Shepherd died at Sunnybrook Hospital on July 24, 1960, with a distinguished military and community service record. His wife passed away in October 1979. Although there are a large number of descendants, there is not one 'Shepherd' to carry on the family name.

It is of interest to note that 20 Chapel Street has been in the Shepherd family for over three generations and was last occupied by Violet Shepherd (Mrs. Jack King).

The author, once married to a great-granddaughter of little "Johnny" Shepherd, has a son, John Anthony Scott McDonald, who can be proud of the fine contribution that the generations of Shepherds made to the community. ∞

EDWARD FLECK AND THE
GEORGETOWN COATED PAPER MILL

Just as he was about to leave Georgetown in 1909 to return to Kalamazoo, Michigan, Fleck was given the opportunity to remain in Georgetown to start a new paper mill with the support of a number of local businessmen. Edward Fleck was an active citizen in his community. He sat on several boards and committees, was the youngest Halton County Warden when he accepted the position for the 1915-1916 term and sat on Georgetown council.

L. Edward Fleck was born at Wabash, Indiana in 1882. His ancestors were of German origin and carried the surname "Von Fleck" before emigrating to the United States in 1822.

Edward took an interest in paper-making during his apprentice years. He studied paper technology at evening courses and subsequently worked for paper companies at Hamilton, Ohio and Kalamazoo, Michigan.

In 1905 when Barber Paper Mills in Georgetown were planning to open a 'coating' mill, Ed Fleck was summoned to Georgetown from Kalamazoo and was the first superintendent of the Barber Coated Mill, which was later known as Provincial Paper and eventually Abitibi.

By 1909 the operation at the Barber Mill was successful and the challenge for this ambitious young man was no longer there, so Edward Fleck decided to return to Kalamazoo. John A. Willoughby drove Fleck to the railway station to purchase a ticket to Michigan but en route an agreement was struck to start a new coated paper mill in Georgetown.

EDWARD FLECK (1882-1961).

It may seem coincidental the new mill was erected directly across the road from the Barber Mill. However, when one considers the proximity to the railroad and station and the fact that Georgetown was a busy railroad terminal at this period, the location of both mills was ideal. Although the mills were actually in competition, the Barber firm supplied some paper to Fleck's mill from the old 'lower' paper mill located on the Credit river at River Drive.

It was in May, 1910, when the Georgetown Coated Paper Mills came into existence. The original building, which has been altered and added to through the years, was sub-contracted by J. B. Mackenzie and was the first building in the area constructed of reinforced concrete. This, like the Barber Coated Mill, was not a paper-making venture. Paper was purchased from other mills and 'coated'. The coating material, a white clay shipped from England, was applied and steam-dried using a roller technique. Edward Fleck developed many roller-drying processes that were later applied in the paper industry in Canada and the United States.

The firm manufactured coated book and litho papers, cardboard and bristol boards and several other coated papers. Two of the first large customers were Laura Secord Chocolates (for their box covers) and *Saturday Night* Magazine.

Officers of the Georgetown Coated Paper Mills included John A. Willoughby, president and Edward Fleck, vice-president. Manager Herbert Gage (brother to Sir William Gage, founder of DRG Stationery which was once situated in Georgetown on Todd Road) sat on the board of directors.

In 1928 the company amalgamated with Howard Smith Papers under the name Alliance Paper Mills and Fleck continued to manage the operation. When Domtar Fine Papers purchased all Howard Smith assets in 1959 the name Howard Smith was retained until the mid-1960s. Domtar ceased operations in 1977 and Label-masters is now operating in the building at 2 Rosetta Street.

Edward Fleck retired in 1947, but quickly accepted an invitation from the Kruger Paper Co. to supervise revamping a mill at Bromptonville, Quebec. Five years after his 'retirement', he supervised Kruger's expansion in Venezuela and two mills were erected there.

Fleck headed the local Victory Bond campaign during the wars and was a charter member of the Willoughby Golf Club (now North Halton). He was a very active Conservative. A great horseman, Fleck owned the second-place runner in the Queen's Plate of 1911.

GEORGETOWN COATED PAPER MILLS, 2 ROSETTA STREET, WAS OPENED MAY, 1910.

Mrs. Fleck, formerly Maude Anderson, was also active in the community. She ran a club for young girls called 'Many Merry Maidens'. Mrs. Fleck also organised the very formal New Year's Eve Ball for many years at the town hall and spearheaded Red Cross activities during the world wars. No one was ever turned away from her soup kitchen kept during the depression years at the Fleck home.

The Flecks were married in 1902 in Indiana. Mrs. Fleck died in 1939. A son, Paul died in 1928 and two sisters Mrs. Clive Snyder (Mildred) and Mrs. Carl Martin (Marie) once lived in Burlington and Milton, respectively.

In 1961, L. Edward Fleck died at Marion, Indiana, only 23 kilometres from his birthplace, while on vacation. ∞

MORRIS SAXE: FROM KIEV TO GEORGETOWN CREAMERY

The Morris Saxe Farm School is an important part of Jewish and Canadian history. The 79 orphans Saxe brought into Canada to the school probably would have perished had they remained in Europe during the Second World War.

Morris Saxe immigrated to Canada in 1902, at the age of 23. Born in Kiev, Russia, in 1879 he lived briefly in England before making Canada his home. One of his first jobs was helping to clean up the aftermath of the great Toronto fire of 1904.

He settled in Acton and worked at the Acton Tanning Company for a number of years. During this time Saxe became interested in the creamery business and took a course in butter-making at the Ontario Agricultural College in Guelph. Subsequently he opened the first creamery in Acton. The business was on the east side of Main Street, immediately north of the Main-Mill intersection.

The Acton business flourished and by 1917 Morris Saxe had established a larger creamery in Georgetown and relocated with his family. The grey block home stood on Mill Street (formerly John) almost opposite the Georgetown Memorial Arena. The side lawn once overlooked the Mill-Guelph Street intersection.

The Georgetown Creamery was on Guelph Street near St. George's Anglican Church. Saxe not only bought cream from local farmers, but also had buying stations all over Ontario. This underlines the fact that Georgetown was a busy railroad terminal. Georgetown Creamery, which was one of the first in the district, had modern machinery for the times, including an ice-making machine.

Fresh butter was sold to local merchants and great quantities were shipped to the Toronto market. Saxe also owned a tannery, knitting-needle firm and operated the first 'moving-picture theatre' in Acton.

Morris Saxe was an avid worker at helping Jewish immigrants into Canada. On one of his farms, the old Eaton farm on the Eighth Line south of Georgetown, he established an agricultural school for new immigrants to gain some knowledge about agriculture. Many men left the school to work on Canadian farms when this type of labour was in great demand. Later, the school became the Canadian Jewish Farm School and was used as a training school for orphans from Poland. The first group of 38 young men arrived in the June of 1927. This scheme, however, collapsed during the depression.

Saxe was the founder and president of the Federation of Jewish Farmers of Ontario. He spoke several languages and during World War One acted as an interpreter for the federal government. He was a founding member of the University Avenue Synagogue in Toronto, which merged with others to form Beth Tzedec Synagogue.

Morris Saxe married his childhood sweetheart from Russia, Dora Gerzog, at Brantford on January 7, 1909. He died July 22, 1965 in Toronto where he had resided after selling business assets in Georgetown in 1953.

Their marriage resulted in the birth of five children: Mina, Pearl, David, Percy and Leona. Mr. And Mrs. Percy Saxe once lived immediately south of Georgetown on part of the Saxe farm. Percy was Executive Vice-President of the Oxford Picture Frame Company in Toronto at the time of his death in March, 1987. ∞

MORRIS AND DORA SAXE AT THE AGRICULTURAL SCHOOL HE FOUNDED ON THE OLD EATON FARM.

GEORGETOWN CREAMERY STAFF IN FRONT OF THE PLANT IN 1920. MORRIS SAXE IS SEATED WEARING THE APRON.

SMITH AND STONE: QUEEN STREET TAILORS TO GEORGETOWN MANUFACTURERS

William Smith was President of the firm and Benny Stone was Vice-President and General Manager. Although Smith was known to visit the plant perhaps only once or twice a year, because of his involvement with Dominion Coal and Wood Co. Ltd., Stone was very active in the Georgetown company's day-to-day operation. Smith and Stone became one of the largest suppliers of electrical wiring devices in the Canadian market and one of Georgetown's largest employers.

William Henry Smith was born in Devon, England in 1868. He immigrated with his parents, William Walford and Margaret Ann Smith, to Canada in approximately 1873. His father worked with the Grand Trunk Railway while his mother operated a boarding house for railway workers near the 'round house' in the east end of Toronto.

William Henry, the eldest of four children, married Sarah Ann Atkinson of Toronto on January 1, 1894. They operated a haberdashery and tailor shop on Queen Street east of Spadina Road and lived above the store. Smith started Dominion Coal and Wood Co. in 1912 on Danforth Avenue in Toronto and eventually opened three branches in the city.

Barnet Stone was born in 'Imperial' Russia in 1882. He relocated to England at about the age of 12. His mother had died at his birth and his father eventually left for the United States.

Barnet, or 'Benny' as he was known, emigrated from England in 1905 and settled in the Kingston area. He later brought his brothers and sisters to Canada. Benny had learned the tailoring business in England and was an apprentice tailor in Kingston. In the early 1910's he set up his own tailor shop on Queen Street in Toronto.

Benny Stone married Henrietta Wynston in 1917. Miss Wynston was born in New York and moved with her family to Toronto at age 13. Her father, A. L. Wynston, was well established in the electrical supply business and owned the Victoria Electric Supply Company. He was a pioneer in the business in Canada and felt that electrical wiring devices should be produced here. It was Wynston who got Benny started in the electric devices business.

Early in World War One, Smith and Stone had worked as tailors on Queen Street making uniforms for Canadian soldiers. Smith gave up tailoring in 1914 to devote more time to Dominion Coal and Wood Limited.

William Smith, Benny Stone and Louis Singer, a Toronto solicitor, in 1919 formed a partnership and

HENRY WILLIAM SMITH (1868-1947).

BARNET STONE (1882-1962).

SMITH AND STONE LTD., GEORGETOWN.

purchased a business in Georgetown known as The Glass Gardens. The firm had been in poor financial shape. With Mr. Wynston's assistance the three men converted the company into an electrical wiring devices manufacturer. On May 7, 1919 the firm Smith and Stone Limited was incorporated. Mr. Wynston, however, did not get involved with the new enterprise and moved to California in 1920.

Benny commuted from Toronto to Georgetown every day, originally by train. During the depression years there was a cutback on train service and with improved roads, he drove each day. The Stones lived in Georgetown for about a year (1924-1925) but returned to Toronto. Their home was on King Street (near McNabb).

Benny Stone and William Smith were great humanitarians. Local people recall getting financial and moral support through various hardships from Mr. Stone. He gave many local new home owners a helping hand and loaned more than one young fellow money for an engagement ring. Mr. Stone was a great supporter of the Georgetown Citizens' Band and an Honorary President of that organization. Henry Smith was active in municipal affairs and fraternal organizations in Toronto. He was a member of the Toronto Board of Education and a devoted supporter of Howard Park United Church.

On May 29, 1944 Messrs. Smith and Stone sold their interest to Duplate Canada Limited. Duplate was headed up by Colonel Phillips and Brigadier Wallace who were both active leaders in developing and researching military supplies during World War Two.

Vice-President of Research Enterprises, a government agency, and a Director of the National Research Council, Brigadier Wallace realized the need for steatite—a very dense ceramic used in the insulation of high-frequency radar. While travelling to Guelph on business the Brigadier stopped to view the Smith and Stone operation, which was equipped to manufacture the badly needed steatite. Under suggestion from C. D. Howe, Minister of Munitions and Supply, Colonel Phillips and Brigadier Wallace purchased the Smith and Stone operation.

The Brigadier moved to Georgetown in 1944 and took up residence on Maple Avenue in a house built (with some interruption) during the Fenian Raids of 1866. The brick home with its double white columns overlooked the North Halton Golf Course. He eventually moved to a 120-hectare estate called Rolling Hills Farm north of Georgetown. Colonel Phillips succumbed to a heart attack in 1964 during a Christmas visit at the Wallaces in Palm Beach, Florida. Brigadier Wallace was then appointed Chairman of Duplate Canada in 1965. He retired three years later.

Smith and Stone Limited was always a leader and pioneer in electrical wiring devices and porcelain manufacturing and was one of the few firms to expand during the depression. Duplate eventually merged with Canadian General Electric Wiring Devices Division. In 1980 the company was for sale and with no interest from potential buyers, the operation was purchased by a group of thirteen employees and six years later was sold to Hammond Manufacturing of Guelph, Ontario. The Smith and Stone plant closed in October, 1992 as a result of depressed housing starts, the recession, NAFTA and labour-management problems.

William Henry Smith died in Toronto in 1947. The Dominion Coal and Wood Co., Ltd. still operates as a family business in Toronto. Benny Stone died in 1962. ✖

J.B. MACKENZIE: BUILDER TO NORTH HALTON

J.B. Mackenzie had many sub-contractors who worked for him over the years and accepted his suggested payment without question, knowing that the deal would be fair. Mackenzie added to or remodelled almost every building on the main streets of both Acton and Georgetown over the years and contracted additions to most schools.

John Boyd Mackenzie was born on the Esquesing-Nassagaweya Town Line, just south of Acton, in 1876. He farmed with his father and eventually started a carpentry and contracting business in Acton, which resulted in the opening of a carpentry shop and planing mill in 1900.

It was 1909 when J. B. Mackenzie bought out the planing business in Georgetown of H. P. Lawson. The original stone planing mill still stands at the corner of James and Draper Streets.

Mackenzie was responsible for the building of many residential and commercial buildings throughout Acton and Georgetown. His first contract in Georgetown was to remodel the livery stables on Mill Street for John A.

J. B. MACKENZIE (1876-1947).

Willoughby. This building is now the home of the Georgetown Branch of the Royal Canadian Legion. The same firm, J.B. Mackenzie and Son, was involved with renovations inside the building when the Legion lounge was installed several years later. Mackenzie also sub-contracted the building of the Georgetown Coated Paper Mills at 2 Rosetta Street, which once housed Domtar Fine Papers and was the first building in the area to be constructed of reinforced concrete.

An ambitious young man, Mackenzie owned both the Acton and Georgetown mills when only 33 years of age. A colourful example of his determination is depicted when the sub-contractors responsible for the placing of the large post office clock in Acton were having difficulties. J.B. came on the scene and offered to do the job. He was able to raise and set the new clock into position by using a series of pulleys and ropes hitched onto his Model T Ford.

One of his contributions to the appearance of Georgetown was the Mackenzie residence known as 'The Birches' at 75 Mill Street which was built in 1915. Willoughby, of real estate fame, contributed this piece of land for the erection of a public library in Georgetown, but when the Congregational Church was deeded for this purpose, Willoughby sold the land to Mackenzie for $500 and gave the money towards the purchase of new books and equipment.

A group of Georgetown businessmen, including Mackenzie, were land speculators. They would purchase tracts of land, subdivide and build. One such venture involved the purchase of the old Georgetown Academy on what is now Academy Road. The plan was to tear down the old brick building and erect some new homes with the material. Apparently an old man who had taken refuge in the building would not leave when served notice. While workmen tore the building apart he sat inside, until the location was extremely hazardous, and played his violin. Two brick houses stand on the corner of Victoria Street and Academy Road were built by Mackenzie from the remains of the old Academy.

Mackenzie also built two buildings which once served as theatres in Georgetown and Acton: The Gregory Theatre on Mill Street, Acton and the Mackenzie Building which housed the Roxy Theatre on Mill Street in Georgetown until a devastating fire in 1958.

The firm also manufactured a small incubator operated by a coal-oil burner. This item could be found on chicken farms from coast to coast during the early 1900's.

In 1907 Mackenzie married a Rockwood girl, Eliza McQueen, who taught primary classes in Acton. They resided at Church and Main Streets in Acton, in a cement

THE ROXY THEATRE, 72 MILL STREET, GEORGETOWN .

block house which he built before the marriage, until moving to Georgetown in 1915.

The Mackenzie firm, one of the oldest in the area, has always been a family concern. J.B's four children all had an interest in their father's business. Daughter Jean served for many years as bookkeeper, while son Sam

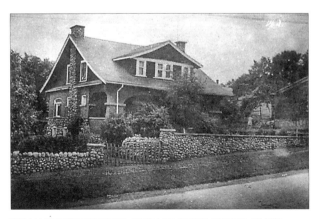

THE MACKENZIE RESIDENCE AT 75 MILL STREET, KNOWN AS 'THE BIRCHES', WAS BUILT IN 1915 AND REMAINED IN THE FAMILY UNTIL 1959.

operated the store and office for many years. Marjory, the younger daughter, a dietician, always gave a helping hand at home. Upon returning from the RCAF in 1945, the younger son Ken managed the Acton branch until his death in 1950.

Mackenzie served many years as a school trustee, water commissioner, member of Georgetown council and as mayor of Georgetown from 1930 to 1933. This was, of course, during the great depression and the days when municipal councillors weren't 'on salary'.

John Boyd Mackenzie died the day after Acton Fall Fair in 1947. He loved to visit the annual fairs in the area and renew old acquaintances. He is remembered for his integrity which is typified in one of his favourite sayings, "A deal isn't a good one unless it works for the two people concerned."

The business was affiliated with Allont and Build All Building Supplies from 1960 and was managed by J. B.'s grandson, Sandy, until its closing in the fall of 1992. The building located at 8 James Street, still owned by the Mackenzies, is now a retail complex. ◈◈◈

WILLIAM BRADLEY AND THE DOMINION SEED HOUSE

William Bradley operated one of the most successful and largest mail-order seed businesses in Canada on a portion of the old Bradley farm in Georgetown. People throughout North America would know that spring was near when the Dominion Seed House catalogue arrived from Georgetown.

James Bradley, a native of Ireland, emigrated to Canada and eventually settled in Glen Williams. James was a millwright by trade and while residing in 'the Glen' he manufactured tool handles and bobbins. In January 1876 he purchased the Bobbin Spool and Turning business from J. Williams, a descendant of the Williams family who founded the village.

During the late 1870's Bradley purchased 80 hectares on the south-eastern limits of the village of Georgetown and called the new home Cedar Vale Farm. In 1888, while he was excavating for a new building on the farm, an embankment caved in and he was fatally injured.

Bradley married Isabelle Hainer on July 23, 1862 and 10 children were the result of this marriage. The youngest, William, born on January 17, 1886, worked as a teller at the Georgetown branch of the Bank of Hamilton (115 Main Street South) which was the first chartered financial institution in Halton County.

To help maintain the family homestead, William gave up his position and stayed home to work the farm. He operated a market garden, growing large crops of strawberries and raspberries and he planted a large orchard on Cedar Vale Farm. Remnants of the orchard can be seen today in Cedar Vale Park.

William Bradley operated the farm until 1923, when the Armenian Relief Association of Canada purchased a large portion of the property. It was on July 1, 1923, that 50 boys orphaned as a result of the Greco-Turkish war arrived in Georgetown. They were brought by Canadian humanitarians and after an orientation period the boys were sent to work on Ontario farms.

The Armenian Boys' Farm continued until 1929 when the United Church of Canada purchased the property for the Georgetown Training School for Girls.

JAMES BRADLEY AND FAMILY POSE AT KAHR'S STUDIO, GEORGETOWN, FOR A 'LIKENESS OF THE FAMILY' ON NOVEMBER 1, 1888. WILLIAM BRADLEY, FOUNDER OF DOMINION SEED HOUSE, IS THE BOY BETWEEN HIS FATHER'S KNEES.

WILLIAM BRADLEY STANDS IN FRONT OF THE DOMINION SEED HOUSE WITH A JOURNALIST IN 1940.

This rehabilitation school operated until 1966. Georgetown bought the lands and buildings in 1967 as a centennial project and opened a community centre with meeting rooms and sports fields situated in a picturesque park. The old Bradley farm name was resurrected when the town named this project the 'Cedar Vale Community Centre'.

By the time William sold the farm in 1923 to the Armenian organisation he had become established in the electrical business. The Bradley-Edwards Electric Company, formed in 1922, promoted and sold 'Campbell's Automatic Rapid Electric Fireless Cooker Ranges'. The range was manufactured in Ohio and could "work right off your home lighting circuit through wall plugs or light sockets giving all the advantages of electricity."

The Bradleys demonstrated the Campbell stove at various centres throughout Ontario and at the Toronto Industrial Exhibition. The Bradley-Edwards Electric Company also sold some of the earliest models of electric vacuum cleaners under the BEE-VAC name. (BEE was an abbreviation of 'Bradley-Edwards Electric Company'.) Early models of mixmasters, Sunbeam coffee makers, health lamps and Schick electric dry-shavers were sold by the firm on a mail order basis. The company operated near the railroad station in the building now occupied by McNally Construction at 1 Elgin Street.

When the business experienced a slow period Bradley started a small seed mail-order operation, mainly to occupy his employees. It flourished and by 1928 he had established what is now the Dominion Seed House, which is situated on a portion of the old Bradley farm.

The Dominion Seed House propagated very few of its own seeds. Contracts were made with growers all over the world for seeds which were sold to Canadian gardeners. The DSH offered a range of uncommon varieties of seeds which weren't available from their competitors. The business was sold to Perron of Montreal in 1993. A garden supply centre operates on the property.

William Bradley was active in the community in which he lived. He served on many organisations, including the Board of Trade, which preceded the Chamber of Commerce. He also sat on Georgetown Council during the 1920's.

Bradley was very active at St. George's Anglican Church where he was choir master, church warden, lay delegate and was responsible for the church's centennial booklet published by the congregation in 1952. He was a keen musician, playing with the Georgetown Citizens' Band. In 1908 he was one of the Lorne Rifles chosen to attend the Quebec Tercentenary celebrations.

William F. Bradley died November 8, 1952, and the many thousands of lovely gardens which the Dominion Seed House is responsible for are a fitting monument to his memory. ∞

BUCK'S: GEORGETOWN'S OLDEST RETAILER

The Buck family has operated a business at the same location, 96 Mill Street, for over 110 years. It is the longest-established business in the community. When Clarence Buck, walked to Limehouse Methodist Church in 1928 to be married by his future father-in-law, Reverend Henry Caldwell, poor Clarence was sprayed by a skunk along the roadside.

It was April, 1881 when James M. Buck opened his butcher shop on Mill Street in the McGibbon Block. He started with one man to help in the shop and a boy with a basket to deliver. By 1913 he had four men employed and kept three horses for the two town delivery routes and one for Glen Williams customers.

James was a dealer in fresh and salt meats, hams, bacon, poultry and game in season. In addition, there would always be a large stock of cooked and cured meats, canned goods, pickles, olives and other such goods.

Of Irish descent, James began his life-long career in the butcher business in his early twenties and 10 years before he married in 1891. The Buck family settled in the Hornby area prior to coming to Georgetown.

When James died in 1923, his son Clarence continued the business. It is said that Clarence was a very determined young man, eager to learn. When his father was sick at one point, Clarence quit high school to tend to the business. On his father's recovery, Clarence returned to high school to complete the last two years in one year.

When Clarence managed the store he expanded the business by adding groceries and sundries around the beginning of the World War Two. He also bought the store property, which up until then had been owned by the McGibbon Hotel.

In 1928 Clarence married Elizabeth Caldwell, the daughter of Limehouse Methodist Church minister Rev. Henry Caldwell who had relocated from the Woodstock area in 1923. It was Elizabeth who carried on the food business when Clarence died in 1947. A partnership was formed with Pat Vance and Jack Teeter in 1950, until in 1964 Jim Buck, Clarence's son, and Pat Vance bought out the others. In June, 1971, Jim Buck bought out his partner. Once again the ownership was solely in the Buck name.

After 91 years in the same location, Buck's Fine Foods closed its doors on May 27, 1972. The only time the store had been closed for any period was for renovations after a fire gutted the store just prior to Christmas in 1950. Even on closing day Buck's carried on the old-style service of making up the orders and delivering them.

Jim Buck (J. M. Buck's grandson) took over the business as a food freezing service. This time, however, the meat comes from a meat-packing company.

The Buck residence was located at the corner of Mill and Guelph Streets (39 Guelph Street). The land was purchased by J. M. Buck from another prominent merchant family in town, the Jacksons. The brick home was built on old foundations by James Buck in 1901.

When the O'Neill Carriage Works (62 and 64 Main Street South) burned in 1920 the Oddfellows who had held their meetings upstairs were forced to find a new meeting place. Also, up to this time the main skating facility was a pond in the 'hollow' near where Silver Creek passes under Guelph Street. It was through public pressure for an arena and a need for a meeting house that the Oddfellows decided to spearhead a campaign for a public arena. The site they chose on Mill Street in 1923 was on the Buck property. Up until then the lot on which the Memorial Arena now sits was a sand pit. (When the town converted from wooden to cement sidewalks most of the sand required came from this pit at 10¢ a cubic yard.)

J. M. BUCK OPENED HIS BUTCHER SHOP AT 96 MILL STREET IN 1881.

CLARENCE BUCK BEHIND THE COUNTER AT BUCK'S FOOD STORE IN 1923.

With no artificial ice to contend with any unusually warm weather during the winter months, as well as the economic drain of the great depression overshadowing the Oddfellows and the shareholders in this venture, the arena was sold to the town for taxes in the early 1930's.

The Georgetown Lions Club bought the remainder of the Buck estate in 1953. This consisted of the house, which was in turn sold to the Catholic church and now serves as the Rectory of Sacré Coeur Church. The abattoir was located at what is now the community outdoor swimming pool. In the mid-1950's when the Lions Club made plans for the pool, developer Rex Heslop had a large fleet of excavating machinery in town. Free of charge, he levelled the remains of the old slaughterhouse in preparation for the pool excavations and enlarging of parking facilities.

J. M. Buck gave three years' service on the town council and was always active in community affairs. He bought a farm just outside the town limits, which he used for grazing cattle and growing feed for his delivery horses. The farm sat directly across Maple Avenue from North Halton Golf and Country Club and is now the site of the Town of Halton Hills Civic Centre. ∞

JAMES BALLANTINE: ECHOES OF AN IMPERIAL WAR

A half-day holiday was declared in Georgetown when Lieutenant Ballantine returned in January, 1901 from the Boer War. The Regimental Band played 'Home Sweet Home' and when he appeared on the rear platform of the railroad car in his khaki uniform, a great cheer went up from the crowd. Ballantine was presented with a handsome gold watch by Major John R. Barber, M.P.P. and an envelope containing about $100. But the crowd did not hear from their hero: Lieutenant Ballantine had such a severe cold that he was not able to speak.

One of the war heroes of the Georgetown area was Colonel James M. Ballantine. His father, John Ballantine, was born in County Tyrone, Ireland in 1843. He emigrated to Canada about 1861, eventually settling in Esquesing Township near Ashgrove. He was in the logging business and his teams of horses were well known in the area. Ballantine moved to Georgetown to operate a coal and wood business and later became active in the building industry. Several houses in the King and Queen Street area, some with mansard roofs, attest to John Ballantine's construction abilities.

John Ballantine married Mary Margaret McNab at Ashgrove in 1869. She was born in 1847 in Owen Sound and was a descendant of the United Empire Loyalist family who settled Norval in the 1820's. Her grandfather and family emigrated from Vermont after the American Revolution and settled on the Credit River. The community was called 'McNabville' until 1840. John Ballantine died on March 29, 1930.

James McNab Ballantine, better known locally as 'Colonel Jim', was born September 3, 1876 in Ashgrove. Always interested in the militia, James received his military training in Toronto and Hayland Island, Hythe and Aldershot in England. On April 4, 1894 Ballantine graduated from a military school in Toronto.

When the Boer War broke out in South Africa in 1899, Ballantine, a member of the Halton's 20th Rifles, was one of the first men in the area to enlist. The Georgetown school principal had all the students stand on a hill at the rear of the school waving hundreds of flags as Ballantine's train went past. He acknowledged the ovation from the railroad car steps.

During World War One he served as the temporary commander of the 4th Battalion of the Canadian Expeditionary Force. While taking command during some fierce fighting at St. Julien, Belgium, Ballantine was

THE CROWD ESTIMATED AT 2 000 INCLUDING SCHOOL CHILDREN AND A MILITARY BAND AWAIT COLONEL BALLANTINE AT GEORGETOWN STATION.

badly wounded in both shoulders by the bursting of a shrapnel shell. Also he had been hit in the left upper arm and spinal nerve and his left arm was temporarily paralyzed. Bulletins were posted on Georgetown's Main Street giving Ballantine's condition on a regular basis. In this terrible battle 20 out of 24 officers of the battalion were lost.

His gallantry won him the Distinguished Service Order and he was received at Buckingham Palace on May 20, 1915 by George V. The D.S.O. document, still in the family, is signed by Winston Churchill whose title reads "Principal Secretary of State, having the Department of War for the time being".

When Ballantine returned home wounded a crowd estimated at 2 000 greeted him at the Georgetown Station. A large procession headed by the Glen Williams Band, school children with flags, the 20th Regiment Band, Boy Scouts and members of the 4th Battalion in training, marched to the Georgetown Park for a gala reception.

Edward Fleck, Reeve of the village, drove Ballantine and his wife (the former Minnie Barber, whom he had married in 1905) and his proud parents in his automobile in the parade.

He was an invalid at home in Georgetown for only a short time, Sir Sam Hughes offering Ballantine the command of the 76th Battalion. He accepted and organized and trained the men in Camp Borden. President Bryan of Colgate University, New York, who was seeking a military man to head the Military Sciences Department, visited Camp Borden and became acquainted with Ballantine, who in turn was hoping to secure such a position. In 1917 he was appointed Director and remained on the teaching staff for 16 years. He also coached lacrosse, soccer and boxing teams.

When Ballantine returned to Georgetown in the mid-1930's he built an estate north of Georgetown near Silvercreek. The estate was called Saxifrage, after the low-spreading plants which grew in the rocky area. Mrs. Ballantine died June 26, 1962 and stepson Fred was the last Ballantine to reside there in 1969.

The Colonel wrote a book outlining the history of the 76th Battalion which he had helped organize. He was chairman of the Georgetown centennial committee in 1937, which recognized the naming of the community and was active in the Lions Club and once served as President.

Ballantine was honoured by Lord Baden Powell for

THE PARADE MARCHES FROM THE RAILROAD STATION TO THE PARK. THIS VIEW SHOWS GUELPH STREET LOOKING EAST AT MILL. THE HIGH SCHOOL IS AT THE TOP CENTRE.

COLONEL BALLANTINE AND FAMILY ARRIVE AT GEORGETOWN PARK IN EDWARD FLECK'S CAR. THE ARMOURY DOMINATES THE REAR CENTRE.

his contributions to the Boy Scout movement. He introduced scouting to Georgetown, was active in St. John's United Church and was President of the Georgetown Red Cross Society.

Colonel James Ballantine died at his estate on January 7, 1948. A full military funeral took place with three volleys by a firing party of Lorne Scots. Members of his regiment placed a poppy on his casket and a lament and Reveille were sounded. ∞

SAM MCGIBBON'S HOTEL:
A GEORGETOWN LANDMARK

A meeting place for businessmen, the Georgetown home for travelling salesmen and the hotel which hosted Georgetown societies' receptions, the McGibbon Hotel has been a landmark in downtown Georgetown for over a century. When the annual 'Drummers' Snack' was held in town during the 1920's 'the McGibbon' was the focal point of the celebration.

Samuel Hopkins McGibbon was born March 26, 1865 at Mansewood, near Milton. His grandfather, John McGibbon, immigrated from Perthshire, Scotland in 1831 and settled in Esquesing Township near 'the Scotch Block'.

Sam's father, also named John, was a prominent farmer in the area and a staunch Conservative. John McGibbon, the younger, served on Esquesing Township council as Deputy Reeve and Reeve and in 1909 was named Warden of Halton county.

Sam McGibbon married Ann Darling, also of Esquesing pioneer stock. After their marriage in 1887 the McGibbons lived at Centreville, a community which

no longer exists, situated immediately south of Norval. The couple spent a few years in Acton prior to moving to Georgetown in 1895.

Sam's brother John McGibbon owned the Milton Inn and on May 13, 1895 the McGibbon brothers leased, in partnership, Thomas Clark's Hotel in Georgetown for $600 a year. The hotel, known as Hotel McGibbon since 1895, was originally built by Robert Jones and was sold to Clark about 1867.

A double veranda graced the Main and Mill Street sides of the building until the hotel was ravaged by fire in the 1880's. After the fire a third floor was added to a part of the building.

The hotel, situated in the heart of the village's business district at 79 Main Street South, always attracted 'travellers' (or sales representatives). The 'Drummers' Snack', which was a summer occasion for travelling salesmen to meet socially, was held in Georgetown and the McGibbon Hotel was the headquarters. The Union Bus delivered passengers to and from the railroad station and a sample room was maintained for the 'travellers' to display their merchandise in the hotel.

First-class stable accommodation was to be found at the rear of the buidling. A complex of buildings asso-

HAZEL MCGIBBON (CENTRE WITH MAPLE WREATH) CELEBRATES HER BIRTHDAY AT GEORGETOWN PARK. SAM AND MRS. MCGIBBON STAND IN THE REAR CENTRE.

CLARK'S HOTEL (NOW THE MCGIBBON) AS SHOWN IN THE HALTON COUNTY ATLAS OF 1877.

ciated with the hotel included an ice house which stored ice cut from the old Barber pond and, later, from Lawson's pond in Stewarttown. Fresh eggs and milk arrived daily at the hotel from a farm which Sam McGibbon owned on the southern fringes of Stewart-town. Several shops once occupied the front of the hotel and a barbershop located on the Mill Street side of the hotel, on a basement level, was reputed to be a favourite gambling spot.

If a shopkeeper couldn't pay the rent, Sam would make easy arrangements. Sam gave freely to worthy causes and always endeavoured to help those less fortunate. He took a great interest in sports and was manager of the Georgetown Lacrosse team when they won the Ontario championship in 1895-1896.

The Liquor License Act issued in May 1906 in Ontario indicated that 'bars may be open at 6 a.m., but shall close at 10 p.m. in the townships and 11 p.m. in towns and cities'. Bartenders in towns paid a $2 fee each year and the Act stipulated.."no bartender's license shall be issued to a woman."!

When prohibition was legislated many hotelkeepers 'bootlegged', but not Sam McGibbon. McGibbon didn't maintain his standard hotel license during the prohibition years.

A 1916 advertisement from *The Georgetown Herald* declares, "If you come to Georgetown, don't fail to call at the McGibbon Hotel. Sam McGibbon will always be found in attendance to make guests thoroughly comfortable."

Sam's wife, Ann, kept white linen in the dining room and the table supplied "with an abundance of food—the best the market affords—which is well cooked and neatly served." The hotel in its earliest years had been a popular location for fashionable wedding receptions and banquets.

The McGibbon family lived at the hotel. A table was maintained for the family in the main dining room and large living quarters were kept on the second floor.

The hotel offered 35 rooms and one section on the third floor was dubbed 'the ram's pasture' as old bachelors and single men were assigned rooms in this area. The commodious bar room in the early years served beer which had been drawn by horse team from Brain's Brewery near Hornby.

Cigars and plugs of tobacco were virtually sold by the wagon load at the hotel during its heyday. Sam was a very 'persuasive talker' if an argument erupted in the bar room, especially on rainy days when local kiln and quarry workers had a day off.

THE MCGIBBON HOTEL IS ADVERTISED AS 'THE TRAVELLERS HOME' IN THIS PHOTO TAKEN PRIOR TO A 'DRUMMERS' SNACK' PARADE.

The McGibbon family took a great pride in the hotel business they had established over the years. When Sam died August 20, 1940 only a few months after his wife's death, a daughter, Gladys, and a son, Jack, took over the business until 1962.

The business was then sold to Isaac Sitzer Investments of Toronto and in 1967—almost 100 years after Thomas Clark had purchased the hotel—Gladbar Hotels Limited of Toronto took possession. George and Nick Markou purchased the hotel December 1978. The business, however, retains the McGibbon name which has been connected with the hotel and downtown business community since 1895. ∞

JOSEPH GIBBONS: THE BARBER
WHO BECAME MAYOR

Joe Gibbons' Main Street barber shop doubled as the mayor's office before the municipality offered one. It was not unusual to see Gibbons run up Main Street with clippers and scissors in hand and a 'half-clipped' customer waiting in the chair while he looked into a citizen's complaint.

Joseph Gibbons was born near Acton in 1890. He was the son of John and Sarah Gibbons who were married in Georgetown on April 5, 1853. John spent most of his life in the Acton area and died there on March 5, 1933.

Joe Gibbons was a barber and apprenticed at Morton's Barber Shop in Acton prior to arrival in Georgetown in 1917. He became a Main Street businessman and shared a barbershop with Freeman Kersey. Gibbons eventually took over the business and operated the shop until 1949. He married a local girl, Hattie Sykes.

Joe Gibbons entered municipal politics as a councillor in 1931. He held that position until 1934 when he ran for mayor and served a 10-year term. After leaving politics for two years he returned in 1946 for one year as councillor and was elected mayor again in 1947. He resigned in 1949 to accept an appointment as the town's assessment commissioner. In 1963 he resigned from that position and re-entered politics with a successful mayoralty campaign.

Gibbons refused to accept the $2 500 salary entitled to the mayor. Heated arguments ensued in the council chambers to determine whether the salary should be shown in the town's financial books. He indicated that "some mayors give their salaries to charity. I'd feel like a hypocrite taking credit and glory for giving away other people's money." Gibbons argued that this was no "eyebrow-raising stunt" and that a precedent was not being set as "more able men than I have served as mayor free in the past."

Gibbons had a sense of the dramatic and was a very controversial and opinionated man. One of his favourite sayings reflects this: "Men fit to be called men should express themselves." He made it known that it was the mayor who conducted council meetings. Gibbons felt that public and press should not be excluded from any meetings. "Public business should be treated as such!"

Joe Gibbons had the distinction of serving as mayor during the celebrations in Georgetown in 1937 which

JOE GIBBONS (CENTRE) OPERATED A BARBER SHOP IN GEORGETOWN FROM 1917 TO 1949. THE MAYOR'S BUSINESS WAS OFTEN CONDUCTED HERE WHILE PATRONS WAITED 'HALF-CLIPPED'.

MAYOR GIBBONS PRESIDES OVER A GEORGETOWN COUNCIL MEETING. (L-R) BILL SMITH, ART SPEIGHT, ERNIE HYDE, BILL HUNTER, JOE GIBBONS, JIM YOUNG, 'STEAMER' EMMERSON, FRED HARRISON, ROY BALLENTINE

recognized the one hundredth anniversary of the naming of the community. He was also Mayor in 1964 when Georgetown celebrated its one hundredth anniversary as a municipality and also during the 1967 Canada Centennial celebrations. He was Mayor at a time when the town had begun to grow again. He was involved with the Heslop and Brumac Developments negotiations. This era saw a tremendous increase in the town's population and a myriad of consequent municipal problems. His first concern was to the citizens of the town and one priority was to not only maintain, but to reduce tax levels.

Mayor Gibbons retired after 18 years in that office and a total of 36 years of municipal experience in Georgetown. He made the announcement on November 12, 1968 to a gathering after a regular council meeting. Eight days later he was dead from a heart attack. He had planned to attend a Hydro Commission meeting the evening of his death.

Joseph Gibbons Public School, Gibbons Place and Joseph Gibbons Memorial Park are named in his honour. ∞

HARRY WRIGHT AND THE EXCHANGE HOTEL

Harry Wright was a good 'talker'. If a dispute erupted in his hotel, he would usually 'escort' the contestants outside before any blows could be delivered. Stories about local gangs (some armed) coming into town and customers lighting cigars with $10 bills are just part of the history of his Exchange Hotel.

Harry Wright was born in Wales and came to Canada with his parents at eight years of age. The Wrights settled in Ontario County and eventually young Harry worked in a Port Credit hotel on a part-time basis, while training as a baker. The part-time work inspired Harry to chose a career in the hotel business. His baking background was a valuable asset in later years.

Harry operated hotels in Richmond Hill and Nobleton. Early in 1913 he learned of a hotel in Georgetown that would possibly be coming on the market. He booked into the Railroad Exchange Hotel next to the railroad station as a 'traveller' and spent an entire week observing the passenger flow at the railroad station and the business district downtown. He obviously saw the potential. Booking out of the hotel at the end of the week, he made an offer to purchase. Wright offered half the asking price in cash and an open mortgage on the balance to the proprietor Jack Kaiser. After some discussion the deal was accepted.

The problem Harry then faced was selling his hotel at Nobleton. When he couldn't get a buyer he petitioned the village council to take it off his hands. The council declined and Harry threatened "you'll buy it within 30 days". He then proceeded to permit soda pop manufacturers and brewing companies to post large tin signs on the front of the hotel, creating an eyesore. The village council bought the hotel before the 30 days had passed!

When Wright took possession of the Railroad Exchange Hotel in June, 1913, he already had nearly 27 years' experience in the hotel business. Eighteen passenger trains passed through town daily: over 100 meals were served in the dining room each day during peak periods. The 11 bedrooms were filled during the Drummers' Snack and Fall Fair weekends.

THE HARRY WRIGHT FAMILY AND THE HIRED HELP ON THE VERANDAH OF THE RAILROAD EXCHANGE HOTEL SHORTLY AFTER HE PURCHASED THE BUSINESS IN 1913.

CEDAR BOUGHS DECORATE THE ENTRANCE TO THE RAILROAD STATION WHILE A GROUP POSES OUTSIDE THE EXCHANGE HOTEL ON DERRY DAY. THIS WAS CELEBRATED ON AUGUST 12 BY THE ROYAL BLACK KNIGHTS OF IRELAND.

The railroad used the hotel after any train accidents in the area. Mrs. Dorothy Hillock, Harry Wright's daughter and present proprietor of the hotel, can recall her mother supplying blankets for stranded passengers who were satisfied to sleep on the floor.

In the early years beer was hauled by horse team from Brain's Brewery near Hornby. Beer and spirits were cooled with ice cut during the winter months from the pond at the old Barber paper mill on the Credit River. The ice was then stored in a building near the livery stable, to the west of the hotel, and was insulated with sawdust.

Wright married Arvilla Beer prior to coming to Georgetown. One of the kitchen workers, a great-aunt to his wife, was named Porter. When local option and prohibition forced the closing of bars, Harry quipped, "You can close my bar, but you'll never take my 'Beer' or 'Porter'!" The dining and hotel rooms and livery stables were maintained during the prohibition years and when the Act was repealed he opened his hotel doors three days before the McGibbon. The

McGibbons didn't retain their standard hotel license during the 'dry' years.

Harry, like most hotelkeepers, was a horse lover. He organized local races at the fairgrounds and prohibited the use of a whip in any of his races. He would sometimes make the riders sit backwards in the sulky during the race. The Exchange Hotel donated the top prize at these races for many years.

A barber shop was once situated in the east portion of the hotel. This shop was later converted to a butcher market when George Granger established a business there after losing his position with Swift's meat packers during the depression. It later became a grocery store operated by two of Wright's daughters, Dorothy and Kay. Kay once operated Kay's Grocery at 86 Guelph Street, near the high school.

Dorothy Wright married Maurice Hillock who worked for many years at Edward Fleck's Coated Paper Mill. The couple eventually took over the hotel. Since Maurice's death in 1967, Mrs. Hillock has continued to operate the hotel with the assistance of her children. ∞

BRAIN'S BREWERY OF HORNBY

The beer available at Brain's Brewery was unlike the beer sold today. John Brain originally made the beer with a high alcohol content, but reluctantly reduced this when the clientele complained. The beer in those days could be kept in an open pail in the cellar for weeks without going flat.

The significance of the hotelier in the history of the Halton area is great when one considers all the hotels, taverns and half-way houses which existed in and around the villages at one time. It is said that along the 37 kilometres of Trafalgar Road between Oakville and Ballinafad, 21 hotels existed.

Few records remain of any breweries serving such a large number of thriving businesses. A brewery under the name Brinkershoff was located near the CNR bridge on what is now Main Street North in Georgetown, but apparently had a short life.

The most celebrated brewery in the County was located a kilometre east of Hornby on the Ninth Line a little north of Steeles Avenue and was known as Brain's Brewery.

John Brain was the son of an English farmer and part-time brewer. He left England in 1823 and went to Pennsylvania for three years. He met and married Kathryn Hand Foster in Philadelphia and eventually moved to and settled on Lot 2, Concession 9, Esquesing Township. Here he and his family cleared the land for farming and for a short time operated a shingle business.

The Brain Brewery resulted from requests of neighbours who knew of John Brain's brewing skills from the 'old country'. The demand grew and by 1832 Brain had built a brewery on the farm site. The first building was made of logs and could handle 300 bushels of grain per year. By 1834 a new brick brewery could make 5 000 barrels of beer a year.

A nearby pond was the source of ice for cooling the beer during the warm months. Stories have been handed down about winter days when ice-cutting was underway on the pond and several pails of beer accompanied the workers. More than once someone fell through an opening in the ice and would be taken back to the boiler room to dry out.

THE BRAIN FAMILY POSE AT THE FAMILY HOMESTEAD ON LOT 2, CONCESSION NINE, ESQUESING.

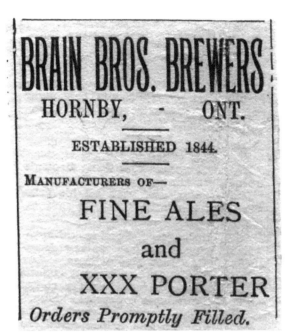

A BRAIN BROS. BREWERY ADVERTISEMENT FROM THE HALTON CONSERVATOR, DECEMBER 1901.

The Brewery had its own cooper who made barrels and kegs which would be hauled by a team of horses to hotels in Acton, Georgetown, Milton, Norval, Glen Williams, Oakville and several other settlements both within and outside the county.

In 1877 there were 10 men and 40 horses at the Brewery. Hops were abundant in nearby Glen Williams, Georgetown and Hornby.

Beer was sold direct from the brewery: there were no Brewers' Retail stores in those days. It was not uncommon for a group of fellows to pool money for a keg or barrel and send someone with a team to Brain's Brewery. Once such a team was returning from the brewery and coming up the Hungry Hollow hill when the tailgate on the wagon broke open and the full barrels cascaded into the valley.

In 1916 when the entire province went under prohibition the brewery closed down and never re-opened after the 1927 repeal. The brewery was eventually sold to Messrs. Kemp and Chisholm who ran the business under the Brain name. Throughout its existence the brewery was always a favourite target for local Temperance groups.

The Brain family was very active in the building of St. Stephen's Anglican church nearby. Even though John Brain was a Congregationalist of deep religious convictions, he joined with his neighbours in hewing trees and sawing logs to form the framework of the church.

All of John Brain's 10 children were baptized and confirmed at St. Stephen's and attended services faithfully all their lives. Reverend Canon William J. Brain, a descendant of John Brain, was the founder and first rector of St. Michael and All Angels Anglican Church on St. Clair Avenue in Toronto. He served there from 1907 until his death in 1931. A window over the alter was dedicated to his memory in 1945.

Bill Brain, a great-grandson of the original settler and brewer John Brain, was the last of the family to make his home in the Hornby area. He moved to a farm near Rockwood in 1968. ∞

WORKMEN AND MEMBERS OF THE BRAIN FAMILY AT THE MAIN BUILDING OF THE BREWERY COMPLEX. IN 1877 THERE WERE 10 MEN AND 40 HORSES EMPLOYED.

TORONTO SUBURBAN 'RADIAL'

*T*he train would stop over a trestle spanning a trout pond and the engineers and crew would cast a line and try their luck. Some passengers would peer out the window, while others would continue their conversations or their reading. This scene was not unknown at Limehouse back in the 1920's.

Although the Toronto Suburban Railway's first car made its inaugural trip through what is now Halton Hills on April 14, 1917, the line actually dates back to the 1890's. The Toronto Suburban Street Railway was incorporated in 1894 and operated as a small suburban street railway between Keele and Dundas Streets in Toronto and Weston. Until 1911, when the line was acquired by railroad contractors Mackenzie and Mann, the railway had less than 15 kilometres of track.

Sir Donald Mann was an Acton boy who became very wealthy through contract work and has become a legendary figure in Canadian railway history. He bought the railway and the extension to Guelph was surveyed in 1911. Construction began in July 1912 and by the following year grading of the line was completed. Although the road bed was built to relatively high standards some sources indicate that the railway was one of the cheapest built lines in the world.

In Georgetown a 96-metre wooden trestle was built spanning Silver Creek from near St. George's Anglican church and crossing Mill Street to an abutment near the former Hydro building.

Work continued on the construction of the line between 1914 and 1917. Although most of the track was laid in this area in 1914, the war effort kept construction at a slow pace. When the track was being laid near the present Remembrance Park a locomotive slipped off the rails and ended up in the heavy mud. A second locomotive was called to remount the engine and used a series of heavy cables and some trees for anchorage while virtually the entire village looked on.

On April 14, 1917 the first car travelled the line and on April 21 the Toronto Suburban Railway was opened for passenger and freight service. The Toronto Suburban Railway stations in the immediate area included Norval, Georgetown, Limehouse, Dolly Varden (known as Scott's Stop), Acton and Blue Springs.

The Norval station at the top of Cemetery Hill was utilized by Noble's Flour Mill. A siding branched down the hill to the mill building which sat just east of the four corners.

The Georgetown station located at 29 Main Street South was a familiar spot for many years. This station was approximately the midpoint on the line between Toronto and Guelph and was an electrical sub-station. Transformers boosted the supply.

If a power failure occurred in Georgetown a request to receive power from Toronto via the Toronto Suburban wires was telephoned to the city. George Davis and George Alcott operated the electrical power house at the rear of the building and both men were relocated to Georgetown by the Toronto Suburban Railway. George Alcott was the father of Gordon Alcott, founder of the Little NHL and for whom the arena is named.

Many local merchants used the freight services to ship and receive goods. An early advertisement indicated "fast freight, same day service". Freight picked up in Toronto in the morning by the Toronto Suburban Railway's motor trucks would be delivered by afternoon at Georgetown, Acton or Guelph and intermediate points.

The Toronto Suburban Railway was well patronized by local residents. Some people can recall trips to Eldorado Park, which still operates and is situated east of Norval. The park, once owned by Toronto Suburban Railway, was opened in 1925 and provided a large amount of passenger business. Based on conversations with the author, it would appear that virtually every child who ever attended a Sunday School between 1925 and 1931 in the Halton Hills area visited Eldorado park!

The Limehouse Station was on the Fifth Line just south of the village and immediately west of the old mill pond over which a curved trestle had been built. The Dolly Varden stop was on the Fourth Line close to the Grand Trunk crossing. It was named 'Scott's Stop' because of its proximity to Ray Scott's farm. The line then continued to Acton where the station stood at 33 Main Street South. The building is now a law office.

The Canadian Northern Railway took control of the Toronto Suburban Railway in September 1918 and due to financial difficulties the line was later acquired (November 15, 1923) by the Toronto Transportation Commission. One month later the Toronto Suburban Railway became an asset of the Canadian National Electric Railways. It was at this time the name Toronto Suburban Railway ceased to be used.

Although electric-powered trains were the transportation rage in the late 1890's in North America, the term 'radial' which was usually applied to the Toronto Suburban Railway, was unique to this area. The term was used to describe the several lines which 'radiated' from Toronto.

BUILDING THE 'RADIAL' TRESTLE OVER LIMEHOUSE MILL POND ABOUT 1915.

line and Car 101 carried the passengers for the last trip. Large crowds gathered at each intersection and station to give a farewell to the train, and heads popped out of windows of homes along the line to get a last glance.

Shortly after the Toronto Suburban Railway ceased operations in 1931, Ed Tyers used the Georgetown station building to house Tyers Milk Products. Doug Brethour operated a dairy from the same building until 1949 when Irwin Noble bought out the Georgetown Dairy and continued the business in the building up to 1956 when he relocated to Guelph and Maple Avenues. The Georgetown Christian Reformed church held services in the building from July 1957 until the sale of the building to Halton and Peel Trust in 1966. The old station was razed to make way for the building now occupied by Canada Trust.

If this 'scribbler' of history could relive the past it would be to ride the Toronto Suburban Radial through the hills of Halton. Those were the days when the radial would stop anywhere along the line and receive or deposit passengers.

Whether you are a rail enthusiast or simply want to spend a pleasant afternoon in the country, the Ontario Electrical Railway Historical Association operates a museum along the original road bed on the Guelph Line directly south of Rockwood. ∞

Due to severe financial difficulties, resulting partly from the increasing popularity of the car, the proximity of the line to the Grand Trunk, motor trucks competing for freight delivery, bus lines being established for passenger travel, and the long distance from the city terminal of the Toronto Suburban Railway to downtown Toronto, the Toronto Suburban Railway closed in August 1931.

With little ceremony the last train made its run from Guelph to Toronto on August 15, 1931. Car number 106 gathered the lamps from the switches on the

TICKET AGENT RAY COLES (LEFT) AND GEORGE ALCOTT (SECOND FROM LEFT) WITH TWO ENGINEERS AT THE GEORGETOWN TORONTO SUBURBAN RAILWAY STATION, CURRENTLY THE SITE OF CANADA TRUST AT 29 MAIN STREET SOUTH.

JOSEPH MOORE AND THE GEORGETOWN HERALD

*O*n reviewing past issues of The Georgetown Herald one would find very few editorials during Joseph Moore's ownership. Rarely did he impress his views on readers. If someone in the village was in minor trouble and Moore wrote an article about it, he wouldn't mention the person's name.

Thomas T. Moore as a young lad came from County Tyrone, Ireland with his mother. He received his education in Toronto and entered the teaching profession, eventually assuming the position of Principal of Acton Public School for over 25 years. He also served as Municipal Clerk and Treasurer of the Village.

Joseph Matheson Moore, third son of Thomas, was born on May 24, 1872. He spent his childhood in Acton and decided early to enter the newspaper and publishing business. He served as apprentice under H. P. Moore, who was editor and publisher with *The Acton Free Press* from 1878 to 1927. (It should be noted that Joseph and H. P. Moore were not related.)

After working as a printer for papers at Bolton, Hanover and Guelph in Ontario, Joseph came to work at *The Georgetown Herald* in 1891 under editor R. D. Warren. He served as a foreman and in a few years he purchased the business and become the editor and publisher while still a young man.

Moore's expertise was in the printing field. In fact, many small-town publishers placed emphasis on the local printing trade and the weekly paper was of secondary importance.

Travelling vaudeville shows would call at the offices and purchase advertising space and seek publicity for an upcoming show, generally held in the town hall. Many prominent entertainers and artists of a former age, including Pauline Johnson, would frequent the *Herald* office and renew their friendships with 'Joe' Moore. Autographed pictures of many well-known entertainers hung in Moore's office.

Moore was involved in the theatre to a degree, when he served as 'interlocutor' or master of ceremonies at minstrel shows held in the town hall. He was a popular speaker and chaired many meetings in the village including the library board. Moore was instrumental in bringing hydro-electric power to the village and was commissioner at the time of his death. He sat on council and served as Reeve of Georgetown.

When Moore came to Georgetown in 1891 the *Herald* was situated over the shop at 67 Main Street

JOSEPH M. MOORE (1872-1939).

South. A fire in 1918 gutted the building and completely destroyed all the former issues of the paper. This was a tremendous loss for the historical records of the town. A large printing press on the second floor crashed through the first floor and into the basement. Joseph had been visiting his mother's home in Acton, with former editor R. D. Warren, and had a rude awakening during the night to discover his business was ablaze.

The paper didn't miss an issue. Temporary quarters were established and H. P. Moore of *The Acton Free Press* arranged publication of the Herald until a new press could be secured. The professional friendship between the two editors was long lasting and they consulted each other regularly. On one occasion Joseph Moore

J. B. MACKENZIE BUILT THIS HOME FOR JOSEPH MOORE IN 1911 AT THE CORNER OF PARK AND CHARLES STREETS. THE MOORES LIVED HERE UNTIL 1945.

JOSEPH MOORE (SEATED CENTRE) ACTED AS 'MISTER INTERLOCUTOR' DURING MINSTREL SHOWS AT THE TOWN HALL.

wittily announced that *The Acton Free Press* was the finest paper between Georgetown and Guelph…failing to mention it was the *only* paper!

A barber shop on the main floor was converted into the *Herald* office during renovations after the fire. In 1952 the paper relocated to 103 Main Street South and then to Guelph Street near Mill.

During his earliest days in Georgetown, Moore boarded at the Bennett House Hotel, which was directly across Main Street from the McGibbon at 78 Main Street South. On September 21, 1896 he married Amy Claridge at the Methodist Church in Acton and the newlyweds made their first home in Georgetown in a house known as Willow Bank at 35 Park Street.

In 1911 Moore commissioned J. B. Mackenzie to build a home at the corner of Charles and Factory Streets. Factory Street, which once ran into the industrial part of the village, is now Park Street. The Moores lived in the brick house at 7 Park Street until 1945.

Joseph Moore died October 30, 1939 and at the funeral his old lacrosse stick was richly garlanded with flowers. Moore had played defence with the AETNA Lacrosse Club, Ontario Champions at the turn of the century.

The paper was purchased by Thomson Newspapers, headed by Lord Thomson of Fleet. The last edition of *The Georgetown Herald* came off the press on July 19, 1992. ⚬⚬

HOWARD WRIGGLESWORTH: CHAPEL STREET SCHOOL PRINCIPAL

Howard Wrigglesworth took great pride in his community. The Georgetown Board of Education named a public school in his memory in 1952 and he is best remembered as a Principal of the much-loved Chapel Street School.

One of the earliest forms of education available to pioneer children was through the Sunday School system. Georgetown and Esquesing districts were no exception, as formal education was not available here until the late 1840's.

The first public school was in two rented rooms in a wooden frame house in the village. By 1858 the school had relocated to the town hall, which stood at the site of the present Volunteer Ambulance building at the corner of Chapel and Guelph Streets.

A large brick building was opened as the Georgetown Academy, a private boarding school. The attendance

HOWARD WRIGGLESWORTH (1910-1950).

was initially encouraging, but the enthusiasm was short-lived and the school closed its doors. The school was situated on Academy Road and demolished by J. B. Mackenzie.

In February, 1859 the Board of Trustees of the Common School in the Village of Georgetown purchased the property and built Georgetown's first public school, known as Chapel Street Public School for many years. The school operated from 1869 until June 1974.

The village of Georgetown became a town in 1922. By the 1950's the population was growing with the post-war boom and the public school board decided to open a second school. About 1951 they purchased property from Jack Tost on Guelph Street (near Maple Avenue). The Board decided to name the new school after Howard Wrigglesworth, the principal at Chapel Street Public School from 1938 to 1950.

Howard Wrigglesworth was born in Hornby on February 5, 1910. The farm he was raised on is now the Hornby Towers Golf Course. His father, Fred Wrigglesworth, was a sportsman and was always interested in youth. He was a great horseman, and showed ponies at the Royal Winter Fair for 50 consecutive years.

Howard Wrigglesworth was one of the best sprinters Halton ever produced and held the Provincial record for the 100-yard dash. He graduated from the Toronto Normal School in 1929 and after teaching in Milton for a few years he relocated to St. Catharines for about six years.

When Wrigglesworth became principal at Chapel Street Public School in 1938, those were the days when there were no secretaries, telephones, copiers or faxes. The principal and teachers practically had to beg for a bottle of ink.

Wrigglesworth was very active in the community. He was Master of The Masonic Lodge in 1948, Sunday School Superintendent at St. John's United Church and was an active director of the Esquesing Agricultural Society.

He received his Bachelor of Arts degree from McMaster University in 1949 by studying during the summers and in the evenings. Howard Wrigglesworth married Ruth Giffen on August 7, 1937 in Hornby. The Giffen family had been Esquesing farmers since 1912.

Howard Cantelon Wrigglesworth died at his home on September 9, 1950 aged only 40. The Wrigglesworth school closed in June 1986 and is now leased by the Halton Board of Education to Holy Cross School. ∞

AN EARLY VIEW OF CHAPEL STREET SCHOOL.

FORMER MAYOR JOHN T. ARMSTRONG AT THE FORMAL CLOSING CEREMONIES FOR CHAPEL STREET PUBLIC SCHOOL.

REX HESLOP: DEVELOPER

When a parcel of land offered to the town for the future site of a hospital was not accepted, developer Rex Heslop gave the proceeds from the sale of a house towards the building fund for the present Georgetown Hospital. Rex Heslop's development on the eastern fringe of Georgetown changed the character of the town for ever.

REX AND EDITH DELMA HESLOP POSE FOR CBC CAMERAS IN 1956 WHEN THE NETWORK FEATURED A PROGRAMME ON THEIR GEORGETOWN HOME.

Rex Wesley Heslop was born on October 10, 1905 in Etobicoke Township on a farm at the site of what is now the Rexdale Shopping Centre. He obtained a Grade eight education and worked with his father in construction. In 1924 he went to Detroit, drove a taxi cab, and later sold cars, becoming one of Michigan's top car salesmen. Heslop returned to Canada and worked in a northern Ontario mine, but moved to Toronto after an injury during a rock slide in 1943.

When Heslop began his own building operation he often worked for other builders to supplement his income. Rex Heslop Homes Ltd. was formed in 1949.

In the early 1950's he acquired over 490 hectares in Etobicoke Township and started construction of the 'Rexdale' area, which was the largest residential development in Canada, with over 2 000 homes and businesses.

In 1953, after scouting the Ontario countryside for a suitable site, Rex Heslop began the Delrex development in Georgetown. His dream was to have a decentralized community with "good streets, recreation areas, industrial park and quiet residential areas." He chose farm land in what was then Esquesing Township on the eastern and southern fringes of Georgetown. Over 720 hectares were optioned and purchased and plans called for 3 600 homes to be built.

In January 1955 construction began on the Delrex development which was intended to attract industry and subsequently create a need for residential areas. The plan was for a self-sufficient community where employees could live near their place of work in attractive surroundings.

During Heslop's development era, builders usually owned several sub-companies which carried out land acquisitions, excavating, maintenance and provided building materials. When Heslop came to Georgetown he brought with him several sub-companies such as Alrex Contracting, Garnett Building Products, Rex Will Construction, which employed many local people and were under his ownership. With the lack of suitable land and an uncertain supply of materials and labour, the building industry now utilizes outside sub-contractors.

More than 2 000 homes were built in the Delrex subdivision but businesses were reluctant to locate in the area. On July 22, 1959 the Delrex Plaza (now Georgetown Market Centre) was opened with seven stores. Many streets in the development are named after relatives and acquaintances of Rex Heslop and local councillors and businessmen during the 1950's.

Original home prices were $11 300 to $11 600 for middle-income buyers and every house was sold with a warranty. Heslop used his powers to press the federal government for a warranty program across Canada to protect the consumer. It was said that Rex was "aware of every leaky faucet in the subdivision."

When Prime Minister Louis St. Laurent toured the Rexdale subdivision he indicated that Heslop had "set an example for the rest of Canada".

Heslop was founder and president of the North Halton Builders Association, Vice President of the National Housing Association, Director of the Toronto Home Builders Association and appealed to Ottawa to adopt a national building code.

Heslop sold the Georgetown development to the McLaughlin Group in 1966 and devoted much of his time to the treatment of liquid waste with radioactive materials.

Rex Heslop, the millionaire who came to Georgetown in 1953 with his dreams of a decentralized community, died on September 30, 1973. He is buried in Metro Toronto overlooking a residential development he built in Rexdale. ◈

AN EARLY VIEW OF GEORGETOWN MARKET CENTRE AND REX HESLOP'S SUBDIVISION PROPERTY TO THE EAST OF GEORGETOWN.

Glen Williams Historical Overview

Situated on the Credit River, Glen Williams is approximately 48 kilometres from Toronto and nestles in a picturesque valley approximately 1 kilometre northeast of Georgetown.

A very strong current on this section of the Credit attracted men with visions of mill sites. It was 1824 when John Butler Muirhead, a barrister in Niagara, was granted 200 acres in this part of Esquesing Township. Muirhead died later that year and was buried in the Butler Burying ground at Niagara-on-the-Lake. Although most history books record 1824 as the date the parcel of land was sold then to Benajah Williams, the Rev. Richard Ruggle records in his book *Down In The Glen* that this transaction didn't take place until November 9, 1825 for £100.

Williams' ancestors were Welsh and his father, Roger,

had emigrated to the colony of New York and supported the British flag and the loyalist cause. By 1796 Benajah had arrived in Upper Canada and settled in Gainsborough Township in the Niagara area. He and his third wife, Elizabeth, raised 15 children. By 1833 Benajah had purchased the neighbouring lot in Esquesing which gave him a 400-acre parcel of land that became Glen Williams.

Benajah was 61 years of age when he bought the property and it was Charles Williams (1811-1889), Benajah's second son by his third wife, who became the leading figure in the community. It was Charles who owned and operated the saw mill and eventually the grist and woollen mills. Charles became known as 'Squire' Williams in this small community which was called 'Williamsburg' by the late 1820's. Charles'

GLEN WILLIAMS VIEWED FROM THE CEMETERY HILL, EARLY 1900'S.

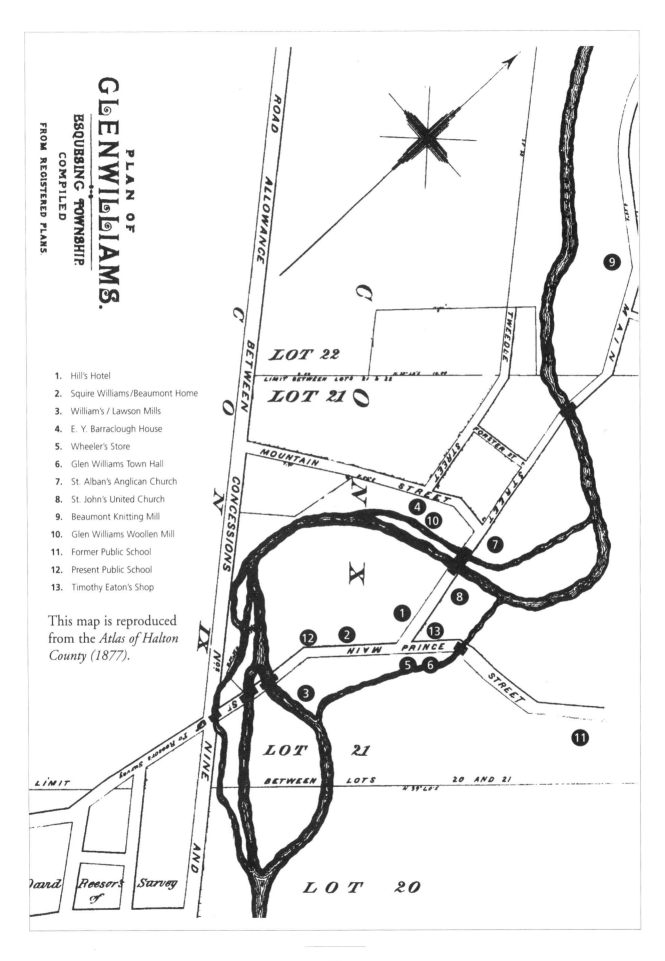

PLAN OF
GLENWILLIAMS.
ESQUESING TOWNSHIP.
COMPILED
FROM REGISTERED PLANS.

1. Hill's Hotel
2. Squire Williams/Beaumont Home
3. William's / Lawson Mills
4. E. Y. Barraclough House
5. Wheeler's Store
6. Glen Williams Town Hall
7. St. Alban's Anglican Church
8. St. John's United Church
9. Beaumont Knitting Mill
10. Glen Williams Woollen Mill
11. Former Public School
12. Present Public School
13. Timothy Eaton's Shop

This map is reproduced from the *Atlas of Halton County (1877)*.

THE GLEN SUFFERED FROM NUMEROUS SPRING FLOODS OVER THE YEARS.

influence in the community was tremendous. He was not only a successful industrialist, but was also named Justice of the Peace and postmaster.

Charles' son Joseph (1844-1920) took over most of the businesses established by his father and grandfather. In 1866 the Williams sawmill was partially lost to a fire, but was rebuilt from local stone. The Williams' woollen businesses suffered not only from another fire in 1875, but also from financial hardship. By 1894 Sykes and Ainsley operated the mill and in 1907 the Glen Williams Woollen Mills Company was established. The Melrose Knitting Company became a subsidiary and operated in the same building until 1949. The warehouse was ruined by yet another fire in 1954.

The Beaumont Knitting Mill established in 1878 by Samuel Beaumont was operated by the family until 1957 when it was sold to Sam Penrice, Gord Graham and Frank Grew. The business closed in 1982, two years after Sam Penrice's death.

Like most villages of similar size with considerable water power, the community had a tannery, saw mills, flour mills, etc., but 'The Glen' had always been well known since its earliest times for its significant wool and knitting industries. Quality brands such as Glenmont (a joining of Glen Williams and Beaumont) were manufactured in the village and sold across Canada.

Large manufacturers like the Toronto Carpet Company were supplied with yarn from 'The Glen'.

The original name of the community, 'Williamsburg', was changed to 'Glen Williams' when the Post Office opened in 1852.

Although never incorporated as a village, Glen Williams did construct its own 'town' hall in May, 1871, which continues as a meeting place to this day. The hall is a brick structure made from local clay. Although brick making was once an important industry on the outskirts of the village, it was local Glen Williams stone which contributed to the construction of some very significant bridges and buildings in the Province, including Queen's Park and Casa Loma in Toronto, the Peace Bridge at Fort Erie, and a number of post offices and churches. Several Glen Williams area men developed their stone-cutting skills at the Logan or Sykes quarries through the years.

As mentioned previously, power for driving the original equipment in the Glen was supplied by the strong current of the Credit River. Eventually dynamos and steam boilers became the sources of power for the mills. The earliest source of hydro power for Georgetown was from the Glen through Joseph Williams and H. P. Lawson, a prominent Georgetown businessman, who had purchased the Williams saw mill. This build-

WORKERS POSE WITH THE GLEN WOOLLEN MILLS TRUCK.

THE GLEN WILLIAMS CITIZEN'S BAND.

GLEN WILLIAMS SCHOOL 1910.

ing later housed Apple Products Ltd. for a number of years and is now part of The Williams Mill Creative Arts Studio owned by Doug Brock of Georgetown.

The focal point in the village was the general store. In the Glen, the Wheeler's Store was often considered the community meeting place and would be visited most days because the post office was located in the store. Timothy Eaton, the man who founded a retail dynasty, worked as a young clerk and bookkeeper at 523 Main Street in Glen Williams shortly after his arrival to Canada in 1854.

The *1877 Atlas of Halton County* indicates that the Glen had "a beautiful and commodious Public School, employing two teachers" on a hill to the east of the village. On October 30, 1950 the Honorable Dana Porter,

Ontario's Minister of Education, officially opened the new school building in the Glen, built by J. B. Mackenzie and Son from Georgetown.

The same water power that attracted the earliest settlers as a source of industrial power in the Glen was at times a very real hazard. Throughout the years the hamlet suffered from floods during spring thaw when ice jammed the Credit. Through modern flood control methods this problem has been alleviated.

With the large industrial concerns long gone, Glen Williams was transformed into a location for antique shops, craft boutiques and artisans during the 1970's. The community has hosted the official Canada Day celebrations for the entire area since 1976. ∞

WHEN THE BISHOP REFUSED TO ATTEND THE LAYING OF THE CORNERSTONE AT ST. ALBAN'S ANGLICAN CHURCH IN SEPTEMBER 1902, JUDGE JOHN E. HARDING, MASTER OF THE MASONIC LODGE, OFFICIATED.

WHEELER'S STORE: GLEN FOCAL POINT

If two children came into the Wheeler store and only one had money, often they would both leave with some candy or ice cream. The village children certainly lost a friend when Harold Wheeler died in 1971.

Usually the hub of any community in early times was the general store, much like modern plazas are today. The general store was not merely the place you could buy a pair of trousers, a bag of jelly beans for a nickel or some stove polish, it was also a community centre where meetings were held after supper or after the chores were done. A storekeeper was someone you could talk to because you probably knew as much about his family and background as he did yours. This approachable manner was not uncommon at the store in the Glen known as Wheeler's.

Andrew Wheeler worked for a John Moore in Limehouse managing a sawmill before moving to Glen Williams in 1883 and purchasing the store and post office. The familiar red brick store at 517 Main Street was built by Charles Williams in the late 1830's of hand-made brick. The walls are three bricks thick and the beams two feet square. The building was sold to Mr. McCrea who was appointed village postmaster and later sold to Andrew Wheeler. He was remembered as a fine old gentleman who loved to talk of the old days and share a story with the customers. Andrew wore a goatee which he would tug at all day while leaning over the large counter in the middle of the store.

John Alexander Wheeler, born at Limehouse in 1874, was almost 10 when his father Andrew bought the store and therefore had an opportunity to grow up with the business which he took over in 1912. He is well remembered for his musical talents and more especially for his avid interest in photography. Many of the better historical photographs not only of Glen Williams but of the region are by John A. Wheeler. If there was a garden party at the Beaumonts, a group of soldiers returning home from World War One, or a spring flood in the Glen, John A. would be on the scene with his camera.

The Wheeler store carried dry goods, groceries, footwear, hardware, patent medicines, confectionery, fruit and vegetables. There was never any 'bargain' at Wheeler's Store, which served not only the village but also the surrounding farm community. John A. offered his goods at prices that he believed were fair and right and therefore there was no need for any gimmicks.

JOHN A. AND MRS. WHEELER.

HAROLD WHEELER (1906-1971).

WHEELER'S STORE IS LOCATED AT THE TOP CENTRE OF THIS MAIN STREET PHOTOGRAPH. HILL'S HOTEL IS ON THE RIGHT.

In 1944 John A. Wheeler's son Harold took over the business. John A. did not retire but instead opened up an ice cream parlour which was formerly a general store owned by 'Slick' Lyons at 523 Main Street. This white building, just around the corner from the former Wheeler General Store is the one in which Timothy Eaton worked as a bookkeeper-clerk in the mid-1850's.

Harold Wheeler was born in the village in 1906 and was raised in the store, which he owned until his death in 1971. He was the third generation of the family to be the postmaster of the village and is remembered, as were his father and grandfather, for his kindness to customers, especially children. There are many long-time residents of the Glen who can remember the kindness of the Wheeler family. If a child injured himself playing, he didn't have to run home, but could go to Wheeler's for treatment.

Harold was active from an early age in music and belonged to the Georgetown Citizens' Band and the Lorne Scots Band and attended many competitions with these groups at the Canadian National Exhibition in Toronto.

Harold Wheeler married Irene (Nan) Tost whose family roots are very deep in the area. Her great-great-grandfather was George Kennedy, founder of Georgetown. Nan took over the business until 1972 when Charles Bush and his wife operated the store under the Wheeler name.

In December 1973, Mel Smith opened Mel's Antiques which offered the same items Andrew Wheeler might have sold in the 1890's. The building has changed ownership a number of times in recent years, but has been known as The Copper Kettle Pub since 1987.

The Wheeler family is still in business in the Glen. Harold's eldest son Bill owns Wheeler's Haulage. The family's interest in music has been handed own to the present generation: both Wheeler boys, Bill and Marty, played with local bands before their teens. ∞

BEAUMONT KNITTING OF GLEN WILLIAMS

*A*rthur Beaumont served as a member of the Wartime Prices and Trade Board during World War Two. He represented the heavy hosiery section of the Canadian Woollen and Knitting Goods on the Board.

Samuel Beaumont was born at Holmfirth, Yorkshire, England on April 8, 1840. This was a woollen manufacturing district and he received a very thorough training in the business. At an early age Samuel had charge of one of the largest woollen mills in the district.

Samuel came to Canada in 1870 and held responsible positions at woollen mills in Galt and Ancaster. In 1873 he commenced his own business at Ancaster and during 1875-76 he operated the woollen mills at Kilbride, near Milton. In 1877 Beaumont ran the woollen mills at Norval until his firm was ruined by fire the following year. With very little insurance, he suffered a heavy financial loss and relocated to Glen Williams in 1878.

Glen Williams was long connected with the woollen business. When Samuel bought the Hirst Woollen Mills from George Ross in 1878 he used the power of the Credit River to run the immense water wheel. A 75 horse-power steam engine was kept in reserve in case of emergency.

New Zealand wool was used in the Beaumont mill because of its finer and more uniform quality compared with the Canadian product. The Beaumont firm did its own spinning and carding. Products from the mill included knitted underwear, yarns, woollen blankets and high-grade ladies' and gentlemens' worsted cashmere hosiery. Samuel Beaumont travelled to England on three occasions to purchase equipment for the mill. A glove-making business was purchased by the Beaumonts in 1906 from the Dominion Glove Works, which had been established in the Glen in 1881.

Samuel Beaumont married Emma Harpin, a member of a prominent family in Yorkshire, England. They had six sons: Joseph, Fred, Lindley, William, George and Mathew. Two daughters died in infancy. The sons took an active part in the business and were raised in the Samuel Beaumont residence next to the mill. The house, which once hosted church picnics on the large front lawns, is at 580 Main Street.

Samuel Beaumont died on March 21, 1906. Joseph,

BEAUMONT KNITTING COMPANY, GLEN WILLIAMS.

THE HOME JOSEPH BEAUMONT PURCHASED FROM 'SQUIRE' WILLIAMS IN 1910 AT 514 MAIN STREET, GLEN WILLIAMS.

the eldest son, controlled the business from 1885 until his death in 1943. Joseph, like his father, was very active in the Anglican Church in Georgetown and Glen Williams. He was involved with the plans to build an Anglican Church in the Glen against the wishes of Bishop Du Moulin who felt that St. George's Anglican Church in Georgetown was sufficient to serve local Anglicans. Both Samuel and Joseph were members of the Masonic Lodge which was invited to lay the corner stone at St. Alban's Anglican Church when it was opened June 24, 1903 in the Glen. Bishop Du Moulin did, however, consecrate the church six years later.

Joseph Beaumont married Janet Cooper and raised a family of five: Winifred, Harold (Tom), Arthur, Harpin and Eleanor, in a house at the corner of Joseph and Main Street in the Glen. The Manor House at 514 Main Street was purchased from Squire Williams in 1910 and each Beaumont child took an active interest in the mill.

The second eldest son, Arthur, married Marie Graham and eventually took over the business at the time of his father's death in 1943. Arthur was a charter member and past president of the Georgetown Lions Club. He

continued the family ties with the Anglican Church and served as Warden of St. Alban's in the Glen for 30 years. Marie Beaumont operates an antiques shop in the Manor House situated in the heart of the village. Her shop specializes in Canadian pine furniture.

A plaque was erected in St. Alban's Anglican Church in June, 1976 in memory of Arthur Beaumont who, like his ancestors, had a great love for his church and village.

Beaumont sold the mill in 1957 to Sam Penrice, Gord Graham and Frank Grew. Penrice and Graham operated the business after Mr. Grew died in a plane crash in 1959. On May 1st, 1974 Doug Penrice, Sam's son, replaced Graham as the equal partner. When Sam died in 1980 his children, Doug and Jean, continued the business, which sold heavy work socks across Canada and on a limited basis in the United States and Britain. In November, 1982 the business was purchased by Hanson-Mohawk of Hull, Quebec. This company was only interested in the equipment and not the building, so Penrice continued a retail outlet in the old Beaumont Knitting Mill until 1985 along with some craft boutiques. ✖

T. J. HILL AND
THE HORSE IN THE BAR

The bar was considered one of the best in the area. A pint glass of beer could be had for a nickel, and those were the days when you could go to the hotel and fill a five-pound honey pail with beer.

Thomas Jefferson Hill, named after an author of the Declaration of Independence and President of the United States, was born in Kentucky in 1855. At the age of 11 he ran away with the circus and eventually chose cabinet making as his trade and worked in Toronto. Hill then entered the hotel business in Toronto and at one time owned the Gladstone Hotel which stands at the corner of Queen and Dufferin Streets.

Hill came to Glen Williams about 1906 and purchased The Glen Hotel from Timothy Cunningham. The hotel at 524 Main Street had 12 bedrooms, a dining room, bar and stables for 15 horses. Every room had its own wash basin, water pitcher, soap dish and brass bed. Accommodation was $2 a night, which included a hot breakfast. The hotel is on the right of the photograph on page 75.

The beer was probably from Brain's Brewery in Hornby, which was the main supplier for the local hotels. There were no sophisticated refrigerator systems at the time Hill operated the hotel: beer was kept 'chilled' in the naturally cool cellar. The only cooling system was the ice box refrigerator with a two-block capacity and glass doors.

The three draft taps used to draw beer were apparently well utilized, especially Friday and Saturday nights when the crews from the Logan and Hurst quarries came into the village to add another episode to their feud. A strip of wood is still missing from the banister inside the old hotel from the night T. J. 'escorted' an over-anxious patron out the door.

Hill's hotel exceeded all standards a hotel had to meet in those days. Hotel and tavern proprietors today have the Ontario Liquor Control Board to contend with, but even back then periodic checks were made by government representatives. One Sunday afternoon an officer and his driver pulled up in front of the Beaumont residence, around the corner from the hotel. The driver was sent in to purchase a box of cigars. When the driver returned to the car with cigars, T. J. was charged with opening his bar on Sunday. The charge was withdrawn and T. J. retained his integrity when it was revealed the cigars were given to the driver and no sale had taken place!

Hill was a physically large man and was always active in various sports. He belonged to the Toronto Scullers Club and his obituary notice recorded that he won a race against the famous marathon runner Tom Longboat on Toronto Island. His first love was horses. T. J. was the official starter for a number of years at the Dufferin race track in Toronto and at the local fairs. His stables at the Glen Hotel were used by Seagram Distillers to house their potential runners for the Queen's Plate. They were trained by Hill at a farm near the present Sheridan Nurseries site on the Town Line. T. J. had his own favourite trotter, 'Black Diamond', which he ran in many races. He also took pride in his two Black Labradors used for hunting. He was a founding member of the Caledon Fish Club.

Prior to his arrival in the Glen, T. J. was a militia sergeant with the York Rifles and was presented with a medal for his service during the Northwest Rebellion

T.J. HILL (1855-1935).

T.J. HILL WAS A GREAT HORSE-LOVER: HE EVEN INVITED A HORSE AND SULKY FROM TIME TO TIME INTO HIS BAR.

in 1885. He was a member of Masonic Lodges in Toronto and locally. T. J. Hill was never active in politics but was a very staunch Conservative. It is said that during one election the Tories won in the Glen by one vote and the last man to cast his ballot was T. J. who had gone to the polls on crutches.

The Glen Hotel ceased business when prohibition was declared. Hill continued with his cabinet-making and operated a boarding house in the hotel building. When prohibition was repealed in 1927 the Glen Hotel didn't resume business. Apparently temperance groups in the area were prepared to petition against the reopening.

Hill died at his hotel in July, 1935 at the age of 80. Hill had married a young Welsh girl, Gertrude Hewitt, who came to Canada in 1904. His widow moved to Tweedle Street and sold the hotel building, which remains a private residence. Gertrude, who sang in St. Alban's Anglican church choir for many years, died on December 5, 1942. She was active in the operation of the hotel and supervised 'the help' and worked in the kitchen.

Tom Hill, a son, was the first mayor of the Town of Halton Hills and served in the Mayor's office from 1974 to 1978. He entered politics in 1963 when he sat on Esquesing Township Council for three years, served a further two years as Deputy Reeve and then four years as Reeve. Tom Hill died in August, 1983 while a member of town council. ✕✕

Norval Historical Overview

Norval is situated on the Credit River 40 kilometres north-west of Toronto and 3 kilometres east of Georgetown straddling the Halton and Peel Region boundaries. Highway 7 and Winston Churchill Boulevard intersect in the heart of the village.

The community was started by James McNab in 1820. The McNabs were of Scottish ancestry and had settled in Vermont. Being of Scottish loyalist stock the family moved to the Niagara area from Vermont after the American Revolution. Three McNab brothers came to the Halton area in 1820, one (Archibald) farmed in the Scotch Block immediately north of Milton, while James and Alexander saw the potential for mill sites on the Credit River.

In the April 10, 1827 issue of *The Colonial Advocate*, James McNab encouraged skilled tradesmen, including blacksmiths, coopers, carpenters, shoemakers and others to the village he had laid out. He was offering "a quarter of a lot and a free deed of the same and as such require a waterfall to drive their works, will be supplied on reasonable terms". James refers to the place as 'Esquesing Mills', but records show that the settlement became known as 'McNabville' or 'McNab's Village' from its earliest times.

The West Branch of the Credit meets the main river in this area and as a result abundant water power was available. McNab by 1827 had dammed the river and a year later built a grist and saw mill. Shortly after this he was involved in a very serious accident at the mill site when his leg was crushed under a mill stone. The leg had to be amputated above the knee.

In approximately 1830 the McNab mills were leased to John Barnhart. In 1833 General Peter Adamson (1775-1865) purchased the mills. Adamson was a native of Dundee, Scotland and had served in the Portuguese army. He was awarded land in Upper Canada by the British government for his distinguished military service and settled in the Erindale area. In 1845 he leased the former McNab Mills to Gooderham & Worts of distilling fame. By 1859 General Adamson had control of the mills again, but his son-in-law, Colonel Mitchell, was responsible for the day-to-day operation. This venture did not prove to be very successful as the operation was taken over by the Bank of Ontario in the mid-1860's.

Robert Noble (1835-1908) purchased the mills from the Bank in 1868. This transaction brought a new prosperity to the village since the mills had been standing idle for about two years. Noble also purchased 175 hectares of land including the red brick house erected by General Adamson which still stands along the Credit. Robert Noble completely re-equipped the mill and eventually created one of the most successful flour businesses in this part of the country.

Although the name 'McNabville' was used from the 1820's, Norval became accepted for the settlement from about 1833. There has been some dispute over the years as to the origin of the name. One explanation involves John Home's play *Douglas* where a reference is made, "my name is Norval; on the Grampian Hills". Some argue that this could be a reference to Alexander McNab (James's brother) who had sheep on the hills overlooking the settlement. Another possible reason is that a stream called Norval runs through the part of Vermont where the family had originally settled. The name Norval, however, was confirmed when the post office was opened by Colonel William Clay in approximately 1836.

In the early 1850's when the Grand Trunk Railway

NORVAL RAILROAD STATION WAS SITUATED 1.5 KILOMETRES ABOVE THE VILLAGE ON THE TOWN LINE AND SHIPPED MANY BARRELS OF FLOUR FROM NOBLE'S MILL IN THE VILLAGE.

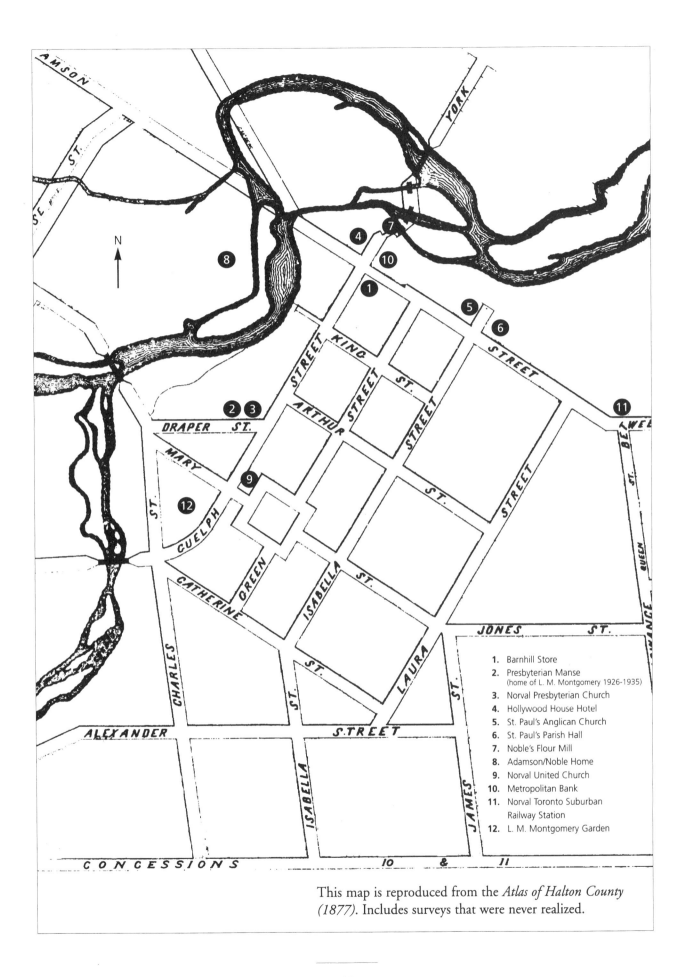

1. Barnhill Store
2. Presbyterian Manse
   (home of L. M. Montgomery 1926-1935)
3. Norval Presbyterian Church
4. Hollywood House Hotel
5. St. Paul's Anglican Church
6. St. Paul's Parish Hall
7. Noble's Flour Mill
8. Adamson/Noble Home
9. Norval United Church
10. Metropolitan Bank
11. Norval Toronto Suburban
    Railway Station
12. L. M. Montgomery Garden

This map is reproduced from the *Atlas of Halton County (1877)*. Includes surveys that were never realized.

DR. WEBSTER (80 YEARS OF AGE) AND LEE WATSON (8 YEARS OLD) IN 1922 AT NORVAL. DR. WEBSTER SERVED AS SHERIFF OF HALTON COUNTY FOR MANY YEARS.

was being planned through the North Halton area, Norval was a thriving community with the various mills in operation and related businesses developing. It was seen as a likely place for a station on the Grand Trunk line. Some area landowners, however, were asking too much for the land for a right-of-way to build the line through the village. The landowners held out and when the final route was decided, it did not pass through the village, resulting in Norval station being approximately 1.5 kilometres north of the settlement. The lack of a station in the village centre took Norval out of the running as a potential economic centre in north Halton. Finished goods, raw materials, livestock, sales representatives and other travellers needed a local railway station.

In 1908 Toronto media reported that 700 barrels of flour daily were being carried to the Grand Trunk station from the Noble Mills. Wheat was brought by the wagon load from the station to the mill and finished flour driven the 1.5 kilometres back to the station. In 1917, when the Toronto Suburban Railway line was built immediately south of the village, the Noble Mills started to ship car loads of flour on this new line rather than using the Grand Trunk exclusively. A siding was built to the mill site. This contributed greatly to the closing of Norval's Grand Trunk Station in 1926.

The Noble Flour Mill was sold in 1923 to W. B. Browne & Co. but was completely gutted by fire on January 28, 1930. The remaining grist mill was destroyed by Hurricane Hazel in October, 1954.

Any history of Norval must mention Samuel Webster (1842-1928). Webster, a native of Ireland, came to Toronto in the mid-1840's, graduated in medicine in 1864 and arrived in Norval in 1865. He not only practised medicine in the village, but was an elected representative in the area for 13 years, having served on Esquesing Township council as councillor, Deputy-Reeve and Reeve. During his last term Webster acted as Reeve of Halton County. When he retired from medicine in 1909, Webster became the Sheriff of Halton County. To my knowledge Dr. Webster was the only physician in Halton to receive the traditional reward of three guineas from Queen Victoria for the successful delivery of triplets. He very proudly had the three guineas made into a fob for his watch and chain. Dr. Webster built the frame home at 505 Guelph Street.

The *1877 Halton County Atlas* shows that the variety of tradesmen and businessmen in Norval matched the needs of the settlement as outlined by James McNab some 50 years before in *The Colonial Advocate*. The *Atlas* mentions three blacksmith shops, a harness maker, carriage shop, bakers and two boot and shoe stores. Two "good hotels" are also listed. These were presumably The Norval House and British American Hotel.

The *Atlas* also mentioned that Norval had a "good brick school with two teachers". This school served the community until a new one was built next door in 1953 by J. B. Mackenzie & Sons of Georgetown. Twenty years later the school became a centre of controversy when the Halton Board of Education threatened to close it. Norval residents were adamant that their children should not be bused out of the community when there was a perfectly good school building and enough students in Norval. The Board eventually did close the Norval School in June 1974. The building is now used as a community and day centre.

Norval almost became the home of Upper Canada College after the turn of the century. Plans to relocate the prestigious school from Toronto were set aside due to World War One, the Depression and then World War

WATSON GROCERIES, GUELPH STREET, NORVAL 1912.

Two. So much work had been done on the Toronto campus the decision was made to stay in the city. The property immediately north of the village owned by the College is used as an outdoor educational facility.

Lucy Maud Montgomery, author of *Anne of Green Gables,* lived in Norval for about nine years. Her husband, Reverend Ewan Macdonald, was minister of Norval Presbyterian Church from 1926 to 1935. Montgomery taught Sunday School and was known to occasionally play the organ at the church. She wrote several novels during her Norval years. The congregation erected a plaque in the church to commemorate this famous Canadian author and her association with the village and church.

Although the Grand Trunk didn't run through the centre of the village, Norval did have the benefit of the Toronto-Guelph road (which was plank at one time) as Main Street. The King's Highway 7 was built through the village—on the original road—in 1920. In the early

1970's, however, some 50 years later, the residents of Norval were not pleased when plans were announced to widen and "straighten the dangerous curves" through the village.

Hydro-electric power was brought to Norval in 1924. Just like Glen Williams, Limehouse and Stewarttown, Norval was never incorporated as a village and continued to be represented by Esquesing Township until regional government in 1974. Norval is now a part of the Town of Halton Hills.

Traces of some of Norval's history disappeared when a part of the dam was washed out by Hurricane Hazel in 1954. The old mill race was completely filled in behind the Hollywood Hotel in 1961 during some road work and the only remnants of the original flour mill were removed during the straightening of the highway in 1973. In October 1970 the post office was relocated to a new location at the four corners with Joan Carter in charge and was closed in October 1990. ⟪⟫

NOBLE'S FLOUR: FAMOUS AROUND THE EMPIRE

The Norval Railroad station was a shipping point for Noble Flour which was mainly sold throughout the Quebec and Maritime regions, England and Scotland and even the West Indies. The mill was always the hub of Norval's industry.

Norval developed from the pioneer enterprise of John McNab and sons, Scottish settlers who came from Vermont in 1820. In fact, the village was called 'McNabsville' until 1836 when the first post office was opened in the community.

James McNab (a son) dammed the Credit River and built a frame grist mill in 1828. This was replaced by a brick structure that stood near the entrance to the Credit Valley Club originally known as the Riviera and more recently Nashville North.

James McNab met with an unfortunate accident soon after the mill's erection. A mill stone slipped and crushed his leg and it had to be amputated above the knee. The mills were then leased to John Barnhart in 1830 but were sold to a General Peter Adamson in 1838. Adamson's son-in-law, Colonel Mitchell, ran the mills. From 1845 to 1859 the grist mill was leased to Gooderham and Worts of the famed distilling families.

Robert Noble, from Carlisle in England and reputed to be the last miller in Canada with faith in the old stone grinding system, bought the grist, saw and woollen mills in 1868 from the Bank of Ontario, which had control of the property by this time.

Robert Noble was well acquainted with the grist business in England. He arrived in Canada in 1852, apprenticing in Dundas and eventually working in mills at Elora and Freelton in managerial positions.

For more than 50 years Robert Noble and his son, Colonel Alexander Noble, steadily increased the flour mill production until the names Noble and Norval became synonymous with Canada's flour industry. In 1880, the Nobles rebuilt the mills and in 1889 changed to the modern roller system. Noble had two elevators for storage of grain—one at the Georgetown and another at the Acton railroad stations.

Some grain was purchased from the prairies but the main supply came from local farmers. It was not unusual to see a string of wagons filled with grain awaiting their turn to weigh-in on the scales at the Noble Flour Mill. The neighbouring Hollywood Hotel was a welcome sight after a dusty ride into the village. A hot full-course meal could be had for 35 cents, which included a thick slab of apple pie.

After 1856 the mill was always serviced by the Grand Trunk Railway which had its station about 1.5 kilometres above the village. A group of landowners asked too much money when plans for the railroad route were being made. Both parties held out, so the railway was put through on the present CNR line north of the village.

Had it not been for the bargaining stalemate between landowners and the GTR, the railroad would have passed closer to the village, thus inviting more industry. In this regard, Norval's industrial potential certainly suffered.

Norval's Grand Trunk Station was closed on July 12, 1926, partly because local farmers had changed from grain growing to dairying or stock raising. By this time modern trucks were being used to transport goods right from the farm to the market and the Toronto Suburban Railway was competing for business.

The Toronto Suburban Railway, which ran just south of Norval on the hill near the cemetery, had a siding direct to the flour mill. Radial freight cars began shipping carloads of flour from the time the TSR first passed through the village in April, 1917.

ALEXANDER NOBLE AND FAMILY IN 1909.

Norval was to have been the new site for Upper Canada College of Toronto around 1910. Over 240 hectares were purchased from the Noble farm, but the outbreak of World War One prevented plans to relocate the college. It took some time to recover from the effects of the war, but the intention was to move once more in 1929. This time the stock market crash put an end to the plans.

In 1934 two residences were added to the Upper School in Toronto, and in 1936 a large gym and pool were built. Sentiment and fiscal constraints resulted in Upper Canada College remaining in Toronto with the Norval property serving as an outdoor educational facility and a reforestation area. To this day, students of Upper Canada College spend a week at a time on the grounds which were once a part of the old Noble Farm.

With the large volume and integrity of his business, Robert Noble provided a banking service for customers until 1907 when a branch of the Farmers' Bank was established in Norval. However, it closed in a short time.

A branch of the Metropolitan Bank was opened on February 6, 1914, at the request and with the influence of Robert Noble. With the decline in business after the sale of the Noble Flour Mill to W. J. Campbell Ltd. in 1919, plus the fact that Upper Canada College had decided not to relocate, the branch closed on April 25, 1931. The bank then amalgamated with the Bank of Nova Scotia. The former bank building, which once housed David Vance's Art Gallery and was a grocery store for many years, sits on the south-east corner of Highway 7 and Adamson Street.

In 1923 the Noble Flour Mill was sold to W. B. Browne and Co. of Toronto by the Bank of Nova Scotia which had taken possession through the failing of W. J. Campbell. The flour mill burned in January 1930 but the grist mill was still in operation up to 1942 under Browne and Co.

The Noble farmhouse, which still stands north of the river, was built by Alexander McNab (another son of John McNab the original settler). The residence was

THE NOBLE FLOUR MILL WAS SITUATED JUST EAST OF THE MAIN INTERSECTION. HIGHWAY 7 NOW RUNS THROUGH THE FORMER SITE AT THE CREDIT RIVER. ON THE LEFT IS THE VILLAGE'S BEST-KNOWN HOSTELRY, THE HOLLYWOOD.

WORKERS AT NOBLE'S FLOUR MILL JULY 1913.

rebuilt by General Adamson in the mid 1800's. The front portion was added to house the guests for his daughter's wedding and was once a complete apartment for Robert Noble's granddaughter, Mrs. Marion Reed until her death in 1980.

In 1924 Alex Noble and his family leased the house and farm to the United Church for a hostel. Young men between the ages of 16 and 19 were brought over from England, Scotland and Wales to work on farms in Ontario and were housed there until placed with a farmer. When the depression set in during the 1930's the United Church could no longer maintain the scheme and the Alex Noble family returned to the farm in 1934.

Robert Noble also served on the local school board as secretary and was a magistrate. His son Alex Noble served as a Lieutenant Colonel of the 20th Halton Rifles, now known as the Lorne Scots. Alex played an important role in keeping the new Presbyterian Church building inside the village when it was erected in 1878, as opposed to having it located on the hill outside the village.

Julian Reed, a great-grandson of Robert Noble, spearheaded the unsuccessful fight to keep Norval Public School open in 1973. He was elected to the Ontario Legislature from 1975 to 1985 and served as Liberal critic for Commercial and Consumer Relations, Energy and Natural Resources in the Peterson government. He has served as the Federal Member of Parliament for Halton-Peel since 1994. Reed still lives on the old Noble farm.

The farm buildings near the old mill pond were always the centre of activity. Old timers can still recall local farmers cutting blocks of ice from the pond deep in winter and loading them onto their sleds to take home for storage under sawdust.

The Noble family and the flour mill both played important roles in the development of the village of Norval. The Noble brand name "Norval" for pastry flour, and "King's Choice" for bread flour, were both known throughout Canada and overseas. ∞

NORVAL'S 'FOUR CORNERS'

Norval's four corners were always the centre not only of the commercial but also the social activity in the village. The mail was picked up there, groceries were purchased and wedding processions would have to pass through the intersection to get to one of the village's churches. The muddy road between Georgetown and Brampton and running through Norval eventually became the paved Highway 7.

This intersection witnessed the heyday and decline of the flour mill, the stage coaches which once ran on the muddy road to and from Toronto (later a plank road), and more recently the widening and straightening of the road wandering through the village.

The commercial businesses in the village have changed ownership many times over the years. On the south-west corner of the intersection stands a business building which served Norval and district as a post office, grocery and hardware store for over a century.

The first postmaster at Norval, Colonel William Clay, occupied this corner for many years. He was a prominent man in the community and was gazetted Colonel after serving as a Captain during the Rebellion of 1837. The Colonel was a member of the first Halton County Council and also represented the area at the district Council which sat for the united counties of Wentworth, Brant and Halton. He served as Reeve of Esquesing Township from 1860-66 and 1871-76 and was Warden of Halton County from 1862-63 and in 1881.

Colonel Clay, a bachelor, acted as a warden of St. Paul's Anglican Church in Norval and was a school trustee and magistrate in the village for a number of years. One historian has noted that Clay would boast that he "never wore a white shirt, never carried a watch and never missed a train." The Colonel served as first postmaster in the village for 45 years until his death in 1885. His successor was a Mr. Vance who later sold the business to William J. Barnhill.

The Barnhill family came to Norval from Meadowvale where William (1867-1907) worked with a Mr. Switzer in the merchant trade. The store in Norval became Barnhill's in 1897 and remained in the family until 1956. At the time William took over the store, little cash was used in the purchase of goods. Farmers would bring eggs, butter and produce to barter. W. J. Barnhill introduced aluminum 5, 10, 15 and 25 cent tokens for farmers who brought in produce but weren't in need of the store goods at the moment.

Most of the dry goods would be shipped to Norval via The Grand Trunk or the Toronto Suburban Railway (the Radial). The same horse team and wagon used to pick up shipments at the stations would also deliver grocery orders to Barnhill customers in the area.

BARNHILL'S
PEEL AND HALTON'S BARGAIN STORE

All We Ask is an Opportunity to lower Your Costs.

Groceries !

12 lbs. yellow sugar for	$1.00
2 lbs Rangoon rice for	.22
2 lbs. Tapioca for	.30
Choice tea in bulk, (black green or mixed) a lb	.48
2 pkgs. Silver Gloss starch for	.24
2 pkgs. corn starch for	.24
7½ lbs of rolled oats for	.49
2 sixteen oz. pkgs. seeded raisins for	.24
1 lb. tin Barnhill's Excelsior baking powder	.24
2 tins canned corn for	.29
2 tins canned peas for	.29
5 gals. American coal oil for	.98

Get Our Price on **"Dominion Tires"** before buying elsewhere.

Canada Food Board License No. S–13324

BARNHILL'S, --- Norval

THIS TYPICAL BARNHILL ADVERTISEMENT (1901) SHOWS THE VARIETY OF ITEMS AVAILABLE AT THE STORE. CUSTOMERS WERE ATTRACTED FROM GEORGETOWN AND BRAMPTON.

The Barnhill store was always a focal point in the village. The post office was at the back and a long counter with a solid oak top ran down the centre of the store. On one side were groceries and on the other would be found dry goods. Coveralls, gloves, work boots, almost everything required for the farm and home could be found on the shelves or in the glass showcase. Patent medicines, cosmetics and various tonics and pills were available in the drug section. The Barnhill store was well patronized not only by the village folk, as old newspaper articles reveal that even Georgetown residents made the trip to Norval to take advantage of Barnhill's special prices.

Many supplies were bought in bulk and along the counter sat wooden bins with roll-out glass covers which contained different types of biscuits. Behind the counter were several large drawers of bulk supplies of nutmeg and other spices.

When William Barnhill died in 1907, his son Everett H. Barnhill (1884-1950) carried on the business until his death. Everett's wife, Jennie Scott (1881-1964) was

LOOKING NORTH AT NORVAL'S FOUR CORNERS.

a schoolteacher in the community for many years. Hardy Barnhill took over the store and post office from his father, Everett, in 1950 and continued the business until the autumn of 1956.

Briefly during the 1920's the store was operated by the Farnell family who also owned the Ballinafad store and later opened a grocery store on Main Street in Georgetown at 102 Main Street South.

After selling the store, Hardy Barnhill worked with Harold Wheeler in Glen Williams for a short time. He was the last Barnhill to make Norval home. He moved to Brampton in 1971.

Wilfred Kirkwood, a native of the Ballinafad area near Georgetown, took possession of the Barnhill store and stock in October, 1956. He learned the hardware business at the Ray Thompson store in Georgetown (at 72 Main Street South) during the 1940's, then worked in Guelph and relocated to Norval in 1953. He operated a hardware business, formerly Carney's Hardware, on the north-west corner of the intersection, until the opportunity arose to acquire the Barnhill store in 1956.

Because he was in the hardware business and required

WILF KIRKWOOD AND HARDY BARNHILL AT THE ENTRANCE TO THE STORE.

more space, Kirkwood resigned as postmaster in the spring of 1957 and dropped the grocery trade by 1959. The office of postmaster was held by Norman Fendley

LOOKING SOUTH AT NORVAL'S FOUR CORNERS. BARNHILL'S STORE IS THE WHITE BUILDING ON THE RIGHT.

for a short time. In 1958 Ormie Carter became post-master. His wife, Joan, later held this position. The Norval post office closed in October 1990.

Kirkwood covered the maple floor with new hard-wood—the old floor had worn badly with the many years of traffic. After nearly 20 years in the village, he closed the hardware shop in December, 1972 and now lives in Limehouse.

George O'Neil bought the building in April 1973, and operates the Inter-County Trophy and Gifts in the premises that has served Norval and district for over a century. ⬥⬥⬥

LUCY MAUD MONTGOMERY: HER YEARS IN NORVAL

"*Norval is so beautiful now that it takes my breath. Those pine hills full of shadows—those river reaches—those bluffs of maple and smooth-trunked beech —with drifts of white blossom everywhere. I love Norval as I have never loved any place save Cavendish. It is as if I had known it all my life—as if I had dreamed young dreams under those pines and walked with my first love down that long perfumed hill.*"

L. M. Montgomery May 26, 1927,
The Manse, Norval.

Lucy Maud Montgomery, one of Canada's most celebrated writers, was born on Prince Edward Island November 30, 1874. Her mother, Clara, died in 1876 and father, Hugh John Montgomery, moved to western Canada and eventually remarried. Maud was raised by her maternal grandparents, Alexander and Lucy Macneill, on their farm at Cavendish on the Island.

An only child, with few friends in a remote location, Maud spent considerable time creating imaginary friends and characters in the surrounding meadows and woods at the farm. At an early age she began writing poetry, stories and started her life-long practice of keeping a journal.

Maud was 21 when she met Reverend Ewan Macdonald, the newly inducted Presbyterian minister at Cavendish. Although she accepted his proposal of marriage in 1906, Maud fulfilled her promise to take care of her ageing grandmother. The marriage vows were not exchanged until July, 1911 when she was 37.

The Rev. Macdonald had relocated to Ontario by the time of their marriage and was minister of the Presbyterian churches at Leaskdale and Zephyr near Uxbridge. In 1925 he was called to minister at Norval and Union Presbyterian churches. These churches have been connected since the mid-1830's. The present brick church in Norval (499 Guelph Street) was opened for worship in February 1879. The stone church at Union, 8 kilometres north of Norval, was completed in 1884.

L. M. MONTGOMERY (1874-1942).

REV. EWAN MACDONALD (1870-1943).

Rev. Macdonald was inducted into both churches in February 1926.

Lucy Maud Montgomery's colourful journals describe their move to Norval as a very sad one. She had become very attached to Leaskdale, especially the library and 'writing room' at the old manse. A dark cloud hung over the Macdonalds during the Norval move due to a judgement against Rev. Macdonald arising out of a 1921 automobile accident. He was himself unable to pay the judgement from his earnings and refused to allow his wife to pay it for him. Attempted garnishees against his salary from the church were unsuccessful, but it is evident from Montgomery's journals that she was obsessed with the constant threat this judgement posed and the chance for scandal and disgrace with the new congregations at Norval and Union.

In February 1926, the Macdonalds travelled by train to Toronto and were met by Ernest Young Barraclough and his wife, Ida. Mr. Barraclough was the General Manager and Secretary-Treasurer of the Glen Williams Woollen Mills. He had come to Canada from England in 1910 and lived in the large brick house at 25 Mountain Street in the Glen that overlooked the mill. Barraclough was also Treasurer of Union Church. The Macdonalds spent their first night in the community at the Barraclough's home. Montgomery's journals reveal that they became immediate and long-lasting friends.

The Selected Journals of L. M. Montgomery (Volume III: 1921-1929) vividly describes the Macdonald family's first impressions of Norval when they arrived by radial from Georgetown during a snow storm on a dreary winter afternoon. The Macdonald family now included two sons, Chester Cameron (1912-1964) and Ewan Stuart (1915-1982). They settled into the community and came to love their new home, the manse at 402 Draper Street, which was built in 1888.

L. M. Montgomery completed five novels in Norval: *Emily's Quest, Magic for Marigold, A Tangled Web, Pat of Silverbush* and *Mistress Pat.* The Norval community was pleased to have an internationally recognized writer in the village. Although she was very much in demand as a speaker in larger centres throughout Canada, Maud never forgot her role as the minister's wife at Norval and Union. She was immersed in both her church and community.

During her nine years in Norval, Lucy Maud Montgomery acted as a Sunday school teacher, hosted numerous church socials, contributed her baking and decorating talents for church bazaars and served on various church committees including the Women's Missionary Society. She helped establish a very successful drama club open to village residents which often performed at St. Paul's Parish Hall on Adamson Street in Norval. At Union she created a dramatic club in 1927 which raised money for some much needed equipment for the church. The old-time costume concerts she organized were among the high points for local residents during the depression years in Norval. L. M. Montgomery was a wonderful story teller, and often appeared on stage at a crowded Parish Hall.

Montgomery's journals not only give a detailed account of the trials and tribulations of a mother raising a family, but she also provides a unique look at people and events in Norval from the period 1926 to 1935. An avid photographer, Montgomery also chronicled this period of time through her pictures of the area.

Maud always kept in contact with family on Prince Edward Island and made regular visits to her beloved home. Her cousin, Myrtle Macneill (1883-1969) had married Ernest Webb (1880-1950) and raised a family of five at Green Gables. It was in the fall of 1927 that daughter Marion Webb (b. 1907) visited Norval and

CHESTER MACDONALD MARRIED LUELLA REID IN 1933. LUELLA WAS THE DAUGHTER OF NORVAL AREA FARMERS ROBERT AND ELLA REID.

eventually moved from Cavendish along with siblings Keith (b. 1909) and Anita (1911-1996). Marion Webb and J. W. Murray Laird (1904-1987) of Norval were married by Rev. Macdonald on October 4, 1935 at the manse. The Lairds were early pioneers in the Norval area and Murray Laird's grandfather and sons built the Presbyterian Church in the village.

Maud was delighted when Marion Webb fell in love with the son of one of the prominent Presbyterian families in the community. Marion is the mother of Elaine Crawford (Mrs. Bob Crawford) of Crawford's on Highway 7 east of the village, which has operated since 1967.

Keith Webb took a job in Pickering, Ontario in 1943 as a herdsman on a dairy farm and then started a successful greenhouse business immediately south of Norval on Winston Churchill Boulevard in 1946. Anita Webb was a housekeeper for L.M. Montgomery at Riverside Drive in Toronto. She worked in a munitions plant during the war years in Toronto and later in institutional kitchens such as Knox College and Willard Hall.

The Webbs, who had been raised in what is now Anne of Green Gables house in Cavendish were partly transplanted to Norval as a result of L. M. Montgomery being there, and they are still there, running businesses in the community. These Webb children would not have been able to take over the family farm in Cavendish because the National Parks Commission expropriated it in 1937 to make it into a golf course and National Park.

Ewan and Maud's elder son, Chester, married Luella Reid in late 1933. Luella was the daughter of Robert Reid and Ella May Hyatt. Both families had farmed in the Norval community for many years and were prominent Presbyterians. The Reids came to the area in the 1840's and at one time owned most of the land to the east and south of Georgetown. Much of the Delrex subdivision is built on former Reid farms.

The Reverend Macdonald suffered from various nervous disorders from his teens. These symptoms continued after the move to Norval and entries in his wife's journal reveal clinical depression and very trying moments during church and social functions. In 1934 he was admitted to Homewood Sanatorium in Guelph for three months. By this time the relationship between the Norval and Union congregations and the minister was strained. In 1934 the area Presbytery had sent a standard letter to all churches reminding officials of the importance of paying ministers in a timely fashion. The Norval Church Session wrongfully assumed that the letter was as a result of a personal complaint launched by Macdonald. The Session had already offered a leave of absence to their minister. By February, the relationship had deteriorated to the point that some of Maud's local activities were affected. Reverend Macdonald resigned both Norval and Union churches in 1935.

L. M. MONTGOMERY HELPED ESTABLISH A DRAMA CLUB IN NORVAL AND PARTICIPATED IN NUMEROUS CONCERTS AT THE ST. PAUL'S PARISH HALL. SHE IS SHOWN, FRONT ROW CENTRE, IN A WIDOW'S DRESS AT AN OLD-FASHIONED COSTUME CONCERT IN 1927.

On April 10, 1935 over 140 members of both Norval and Union Presbyterian churches attended a dinner to say farewell to Ewan Macdonald and his family. E. Y. Barraclough acted as chairman when tributes and presentations were made to Rev. Macdonald. Elwin Townsend read an address to the departing minister and Sam McClure presented the Macdonalds with a 'well filled' purse. The local dramatic society, which she had organized, presented Maud with a desk set. The evening ended with a musical programme.

The Macdonalds moved from Norval to Toronto and purchased 210 Riverside Drive. Financial problems, Ewan's debilitating mental illness, a mother's worry over both of her sons and the outbreak of World War Two all contributed to Maud's depression and nervous condition in the late 1930's and early 1940's. On April 24, 1942, Lucy Maud Montgomery died at her home in Toronto. She had continued to write while in the city and was submitting material to her publisher at the time of her death. Ewan Macdonald died in 1943. Both are buried at Cavendish.

The Norval community has recognized the internationally celebrated author and her husband. In June 1976 a plaque was unveiled at Norval Presbyterian Church by Luella (Macdonald) Viejalinen, a granddaughter. The church choir sang selections from the musical *Anne Of Green Gables* on that day. On October 24, 1992 a memorial plaque at Norval Park was dedicated to Lucy Maud Montgomery by Norval residents and her biographer, Professor Mary Rubio, of the University of Guelph.

To commemorate Lucy Maud Montgomery's birthdate, Norval residents celebrate with an annual

NORVAL PRESBYTERIAN CHURCH.

'Montgomery Christmas' in early December. The village bustles with activities, church bazaars, afternoon teas, and horse and buggy tours. ∞

Acton Historical Overview

Acton is about 56 kilometres north-west of Toronto and 56 kilometres north-east of Hamilton. Halton's most northerly urban community, Acton sits at the junction of Provincial Highways 7 and 25. Black Creek and the Canadian National Railway run through the area.

In 1829 a patent was issued by the Crown to the Canada Company for Lot 28, Third Concession, Esquesing Township and the 200-acre parcel became part of Acton. This community, like the others looked at in this book, did not retain its original name. The settlement was first called 'Danville', a name apparently derived from a young store clerk named Dan who worked for Wheeler Green, owner of the first dry goods store in the area.

The first grocery store (as opposed to dry goods) was operated by Miller Hemstreet who erected the area's first signpost in the vicinity bearing the words "Danville Grocery by Miller Hemstreet". The *1877 Atlas of Halton County* historical summary of Acton refers to Dan as "a clever young man". Gwen Clarke in *Halton's Pages of the Past* suggests that "Dan must have been an up-and-coming young fellow". But nowhere is there a clear indication why the earliest entrepreneurs in the area would name the community after a young store clerk!

On November 1, 1834 a patent for the West Half of Lot 28 containing 100 acres was issued to Ezra Adams. Within a few years the community became known as 'Adamsville', derived from the first real settlers Zenas, Rufas and Ezra Adams. Several street names in the old part of Acton are named after members of the Adams family: John, Wilbur, Fredrick, Ransom, Agnes and Maria.

Another common trait with the other communities dealt with in this book is that when a post office is established, the name of the settlement changes. In 1844 when the post office opened Adamsville became Acton. Robert Swan, a native of Northumberland, England and the first postmaster suggested the name change in honour of Acton, England.

Most local histories indicate that Acton's first industry was McCallum's grist mill. This mill site, however, was some 8 kilometres miles east of the settlement, closer to Georgetown and Limehouse. There is no doubt, however, that McCallum's grist mill, on the Sixth Concession, Esquesing, would have serviced early Acton-area farmers.

The fact that the Grand Trunk Railway ran through the community and had established a station in Acton by 1856 gave the growing settlement a prominence in the area and ensured its growth over nearby rival villages.

Abraham Nelles established a tannery in the settlement in the early 1840's. It was in 1865 that George Beardmore relocated his thriving leather business from Guelph to Acton, and by the mid-1870's his leather operation was one of the largest in the province and eventually reputed to be "the largest tannery in the British Empire". The Beardmore presence in the community confirmed Acton's economic importance in North Halton and attracted a variety of other businesses and trades.

William Hyslop Storey established a tannery and glove-making business in Acton by 1868 which in time employed over 200 and was reported to be the largest work glove manufacturer in the Dominion. Storey was instrumental in having Acton incorporated as a village on January 1, 1874 when the community had a population of 750. He became the first Reeve.

In 1875 the community had its own newspaper, *The Acton Free Press*, which was established by Joseph Hacking on July 1st of that year. A former owner and editor of the *Free Press*, Henry P. Moore, was born in Acton on October 18, 1858. As a young man he worked in his father's stove and shingle mill and later the Moore and Storey tannery. Moore was named Clerk and Treasurer of Acton in 1875 and sat on the school and library boards. In 1911 he was appointed a Justice of the Peace and nine years later was named Police Magistrate for Peel, Halton and Wellington and in 1927 a Judge of Juvenile Courts. The story has been handed down that when H. P. Moore realized one day that he was driving through the streets at 17 mph and the speed limit was only 15 mph, he immediately wrote himself a ticket and paid the fine.

It was through his role as owner and editor of *The Acton Free Press* from 1878 to 1927 that he fought tirelessly for the good of the citizens of Acton. Moore's friendship with Sir Harry Brittain (a member of the

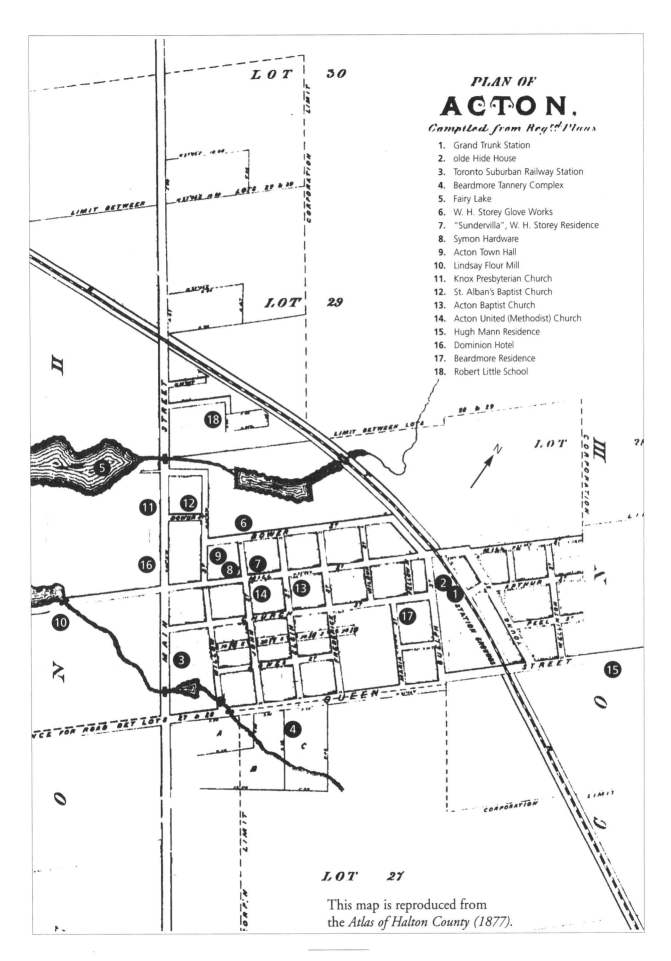

PLAN OF
ACTON.
Compiled from Reg'd Plans

1. Grand Trunk Station
2. olde Hide House
3. Toronto Suburban Railway Station
4. Beardmore Tannery Complex
5. Fairy Lake
6. W. H. Storey Glove Works
7. "Sundervilla", W. H. Storey Residence
8. Symon Hardware
9. Acton Town Hall
10. Lindsay Flour Mill
11. Knox Presbyterian Church
12. St. Alban's Baptist Church
13. Acton Baptist Church
14. Acton United (Methodist) Church
15. Hugh Mann Residence
16. Dominion Hotel
17. Beardmore Residence
18. Robert Little School

This map is reproduced from
the *Atlas of Halton County (1877)*.

British House of Commons), developed while in England in 1924, resulted in Sir Harry visiting Acton in 1931 and presenting the "Floreat Actona" crest to the town. Moore co-authored with G. A. Dills a series of reminiscences about early Acton in the *Free Press* called "The Old Man of The Big Clock Tower". The articles were compiled into book form in 1939 as *Acton's Early Days*.

George Arlof Dills, a long-time resident of Acton, began his apprenticeship with the *Acton Free Press* in 1909 and by 1922 had entered into a partnership with Moore. In 1927 Dills purchased the paper from Moore. His sons David and Jim took over Dills Printing & Publishing Co. Ltd., which had been incorporated in 1954. (It was Dills who published the original *Halton Sketches* in 1976.) The company is now owned by Metroland Printing, Publishing and Distributing Ltd.

Athough the opening of the Grand Trunk Railway in 1856 through Acton was considered a major consideration in the prosperity of the settlement, eventually there was frustration from the community about the poor condition of the station building and access. In July, 1903 a petition was presented to Acton Village Council urging that something be done about the station "which has done duty for half a century". Acton's voice was obviously heard because in July 1905 a new and much larger Grand Trunk Station was opened " of very pleasing design with ticket office, operator's desk, large general waiting and ladies' room at one end and smoking room at the other" according to *The Acton Free Press*. This station served Acton for 68 years until it was eventually sold to the Acton Lions Club, which had plans to relocate it as a town centennial project. This did not happen as the building could not successfully be moved and was sold to Harry McCarthy who salvaged the lumber.

Acton citizens had another reason to be upset with railroad companies when Canadian National's passenger and freight service closed in 1973. Later GO Transit opted to provide a small glass-plated shelter for waiting passengers, but eventually this convenient rail service ceased and now Acton GO passengers are bused to the Georgetown station.

The *1877 Atlas of Halton County* records that Acton had "one of the finest public school houses in the County". In 1871 the principal of Acton Public School, Robert Little, became the Inspector of Public Schools for all of Halton.

In the late 1870's a Professor Kent demonstrated Alexander Graham Bell's telephone invention to an

A PETITION PRESENTED TO ACTON VILLAGE COUNCIL RESULTED IN THE GRAND TRUNK RAILWAY OPENING A NEW AND LARGER STATION IN 1905. THIS RARE PHOTO SHOWS THE OLD AND NEW STATIONS.

audience at the Temperance Hall in Acton. The local Grand Trunk Railway agent, R. Gray, apparently went home and built a crude version of the telephone which could transmit voices over a 4-kilometre area. It was in November 1884 that the line crews of the Bell Telephone Company reached Acton, making the service available for the first time to the community. J. McGarvin was named Bell Telephone Agent and his drugstore became Acton's first telephone office. The Acton Banking Company, *Acton Free Press* and W. H. Storey Glove Works were among the first subscribers.

The original mill pond in Acton, covering 35 hectares, was created to operate the Adams' Mill in approximately 1829. By the late 1870's Sarah Augusta Secord, a resident of Acton most of her life, and according to *Acton's Early Days*, "an educated woman of aesthetic temperament, gradually succeeded in persuading [Acton's] citizens that an expanse of such clear crystal spring water" should not be known merely as "the mill pond" but should have a more dignified name. Mrs. Secord christened it "Fairy Lake", the name it is still known by. Many of the old mill ponds which were once the source of power for the earliest industries in Ontario have disappeared, but Acton citizens continue to enjoy the original pond in a fine recreational setting known as Prospect Park.

The Acton Citizens' Band was originally known as the Acton Cornet Band when organized in 1872. Awards won include first prizes at the Waterloo Music Festival and the Canadian National Exhibition.

Acton continued to grow and prosper after Beardmore and other industrialists came to the area, but by 1881 the Village Council after considerable debate recommended that a Town Hall be built at a cost of between $5 000 to $6 000. The ratepayers were petitioned and

SARAH AUGUSTA SECORD RENAMED THE 'MILL POND' TO 'FAIRY LAKE' IN THE LATE 1870'S. THE CLUB HOUSE WAS ENJOYED BY ACTON RESIDENTS FOR MANY YEARS.

with a large majority in agreement, the spacious Town Hall was completed in 1883 and housed the council chambers, prisoner cells, constable offices and fire hall. The Town Hall was not only a meeting place for official municipal business, but like most town halls of the era, was an entertainment centre for the village and surrounding area. With its large auditorium, the upstairs was ideal for concerts, minstrel shows, and New Year's Eve Balls. In August 1977 a study was completed by architect Patrick Coles which concluded the Hall was in "reasonably sound structural condition for its age". A large fundraising campaign resulted in restoration and repairs to the building. Acton Social Services is presently located in the downstairs. The Fire Department, however, relocated to the Churchill Road South location in 1994.

Any history of Acton should mention that Mazo de la Roche, author of the famous romantic saga of the Whiteoaks family, lived in Acton for a few years as a young girl. Although Mazo's father was landlord of The Stone Hotel the family lived in a house on Main Street (north of Mill). Miss de la Roche was often seen driving around the village with her Shetland pony and two-wheeled cart. Already successful at selling her stories to magazines while she lived in Acton, she eventually wrote 16 novels about The White Oaks of Jalna and sold over 18 million copies. Although she lived in town, she never mentions Acton in her autobiography

Ringing In The Changes. At least two of her novels use Acton settings.

As Acton developed, the village leaders decided to improve various aspects of their community. Electric power had been supplied on a limited basis by a steam generator. In October 1911 the Ontario Hydro Electric Power Commission received a request for an estimate to supply power to the Village. On April 12, 1912 Acton contracted to take 200 horsepower and by January 1913 the first power was delivered to a total of 147 customers, of whom 82 were residential.

In April 1917 the first Toronto Suburban Railway car arrived in Acton. This electric-powered line provided both passenger and freight service between Toronto and Guelph. The Acton station was located at 33 Main Street South. The line, however, only lasted until August 1931. On occasion the cars would stop on the trestle spanning Fairy Lake while the conductor and engineer tried their luck with a fish line while passengers quietly and patiently looked on!

Acton had its own share of grief during the World Wars and the Great Depression of the 1930's. Acton was so successful at selling war bonds that a Mosquito bomber was named after the village during World War Two.

On July 1, 1950 Acton was elevated from 'village' to 'town' status with a population of approximately 2 500. Amos Mason, owner of Mason Knitting, served as Acton's first Mayor.

Acton had its own version of housing for returning veterans of World War Two, northeast of the railroad station. In the 1950's Glen Lea subdivision (south of Highway 7 on the old Mann farm) and Lakeview subdivision (north of Fairy Lake on the old Hemstreet farm) provided housing stock for Acton residents. When the Avro Arrow project was cancelled on February 20, 1959 in Malton, many new homeowners in these subdivisions had to leave their dreams behind.

The first phase of a development by Bovis Corporation, a British-based multinational corporation, was started on the former Seynuck farms in 1972, while the first 76 units of Kingham Estates on part of the Wallace farm on Acton's southern boundary (near Highway 25) enlarged the town's residential stock at the same time. *The Acton Free Press* reported in December 1973 that fifteen of the new Cobblehill Estate homes were sold before the basements were completed.

In March 1964 the Acton Library Board proposed to council that the municipality erect a new library building as the town's official project to mark Canada's Centennial in 1967. The library building was officially

Town Hall, Acton.

THE ACTON TOWN HALL WAS COMPLETED IN 1883.

In the very year that Acton marked its centenary as a corporation, Ontario dissolved the municipality. It was on January 1, 1974 that Acton became part of the new Regional Town of Halton Hills. There had been considerable debate and concern about being absorbed into the same municipal entity as Georgetown with its larger population base.

A number of industries have disappeared in recent times from Acton including Blow Press, Mason Knitting, Baxter Laboratories, Ajax Engineering, Dills Printing and Publishing, Force Electric and H. K. Porter, but none left their mark on the community more than Beardmore & Company whose tannery whistle blew for the last time on September 12, 1986.

The closing of the Beardmore plant didn't mark the end of Acton's long relationship with the leather industry. It was in the summer of 1980 that three Actonians, Fred Dawkins, Ron Heller and Don Dawkins decided to develop a tourism flagship in the town which would recognize Acton's connection with the tanning industry. In November, 1980 'The olde Hide House', a large retail leather goods outlet, opened its doors in a 2 787 square metre brick warehouse built for Beardmore's in 1899 on Eastern Avenue near the site of the former railroad station. The building had housed Mason Knitting, a manufacturer of underwear from the 1930's until 1960, when Frank Heller and Company, another leather company, moved into the building. It was Heller's move to the former Disston saw plant in the summer of 1980 that made the old Beardmore warehouse available.

"It's worth the drive to Acton" is now a well-known phrase and was proposed for radio and television commercials by announcer Stu Holloway. Don Dawkins is now Chairman of 'The olde Hide House' which has attracted over 300 000 visitors on average each year to Acton over the past decade. ∞

opened on June 3, 1967. The first library had been established in 1898 when Ettie Laird, at the age of 16, was named as the village's librarian. The Acton Library was located in the YMCA building and then the Town Hall for many years prior to its move in 1967.

On October 16, 1973, Royal Canadian Legion President Bob Angell and Mayor Les Duby turned the first sod for a new Legion Hall located on the former Cecil Nellis farm on Mill Street near Fairy Lake.

BEARDMORE'S: EARLY LEATHER DAYS IN ACTON

It was not an uncommon sight during the winter in Acton to see 25 or 30 sled loads of hemlock bark coming into town in one long procession, headed for the Beardmore tannery. Beardmore's made the town's name synonymous with leather and in 1944 when the company celebrated its centenary with a large picnic in Acton Park each employee was presented with a new leather coat.

Beardmore and Co., long Acton's major industry, was founded in 1844 at Hamilton by George L. Beardmore and his younger brother Joseph. G. L. Beardmore's diary, however, reveals that he first produced leather as early as 1841. He learned the tanning business in England, in a plant near Liverpool and built the first stone tannery in Canada at Hamilton in 1844.

A few years later Joseph Beardmore died, and after a serious fire in the tannery in 1854, in which all stock was lost, elder brother George moved to Toronto as a leather merchant. He undertook production only on a small scale in premises on the Grand River, until he acquired a plant in Guelph. He continued in Guelph until 1865 when he purchased a tannery in Acton.

The first tannery on the site of the Beardmore facilities on the southern edge of the town was built in 1842 by Abraham Nelles who was succeeded by Edward and Henry Smith.

This concern was bought in 1852 by Coleman and McIntyre of Dundas. They built a large stone addition to the old building, and confined their operations exclusively to the manufacture of sole leather from Spanish hides. During their ownership the building burned down, and was rebuilt. It later became the property of McGloshen and Atcheson who carried on the business for several years, then sold to Sessions, Toby and Co. After lying idle, the entire property was purchased by George L. Beardmore in June 1865. Beardmore repaired and equipped the buildings with the most modern tanning machinery of the time. In 1872 the buildings were razed by fire and through Beardmore's determination were rebuilt and business was as usual within a year. Insurance of only $17 000 covered a small portion of the loss. This time the buildings were built of stone.

An expansion to the Beardmore firm was made in the 1880's when a small wooden plant was purchased, also in Acton, which had previously been used for processing cordovan leather. The purpose of this addition was to turn it over to the manufacture of harness leather. In the 1890's, Beardmore and Co. saw an opening for further development and branched out into the production of belting leather in the small plant.

AN EARLY VIEW OF THE BEARDMORE TANNERY IN ACTON.

GEORGE L. BEARDMORE (1818-1893).

COLONEL A. O. TORRANCE BEARDMORE (1886-1959).

In 1893, George L. Beardmore died and the business was carried on by his four sons. The eldest, W. D. Beardmore, entered the business with his father at 16 years of age and worked his way up until in 1870 he was admitted into partnership. In May 1915 he died and brother George W. Beardmore became the senior partner.

Hemlock bark, an essential ingredient in the tanning business, was becoming harder to secure each year in the Acton area. Farmers were still clearing the land and virtually every hemlock tree cut down in the area furnished bark for the Acton tannery. Farmers came from Esquesing and Nassagaweya, then Erin and Eramosa, until finally bark was carted to Acton from as far away as Garafraxa township, just south of Owen Sound. In time the growing Beardmore tannery used up all the hemlock bark available in the surrounding townships. Bringing bark in by train doubled the price being paid to local farmers. So, about 1879, Beardmore built a tannery at Bracebridge, in the midst of a hemlock region. After a few years the bark in the surrounding area was all used up and the tannery was under the same handicap as at Acton. About 1906 the

Bracebridge tannery was closed and many employees came to Acton.

The Beardmore interests included at one time three subsidiaries of Beardmore and Co., the Acton Tanning Co. Ltd., the Muskoka Leather Co. Ltd., and the Beardmore Belting Co. Ltd. The plant operating under the name Beardmore and Co. was devoted to the production of sole leather. The Muskoka tannery at Bracebridge manufactured hemlock sole leather exclusively, while at the Acton Tanning Company harness and belting leathers were tanned, in addition to chrome sole, upper, case, bag, strap, sandal and other light leathers. The Beardmore Belting Company in Toronto manufactured belts from the product supplied by the Acton Tanning Company.

The main tanneries at Acton had a combined floor space of nearly 92 900 square metres. The Company's farm and employees' houses covered an area of over 200 hectares. Due to the depression and the need to end any duplication of costly services, the Toronto office of Beardmore and Co. on Front Street was consolidated with the Acton offices in November, 1936. A small sales office remained in the city.

Beardmore and Co. were very community conscious and always made provision for the welfare of their employers. Although this relationship was a company tradition, a strike took place in April, 1900 for two weeks after wages were reduced from $1.25 per day to $1.10 due to poor economic conditions.

At one period in its history Acton could certainly have been considered a Beardmore 'Company Town'. As one scheme to reduce employees' living expenses, Beardmore and Co. built 60 homes for their workers and rented them for $6 to $8 per month during the early 1900's.

The Beardmore private residence known as Beverly House was located at the corner of Church and Maria Streets and is now the site of an apartment building at 128 Church Street.

Recreation facilities were always provided not only to Beardmore employees, but to the community. Tennis courts, bowling greens, a large skating rink and a club house were among the recreational contributions. The skating club house, which was on Beardmore property at the foot of Frederick Street, was used rent-free by the Acton branch of the Royal Canadian Legion as their first meeting house in 1931. In 1945 the Legion purchased a building at 21 Main Street North, site of Halton Cable Systems.

The highlight of Beardmore's centennial year in 1944 was a large dinner at the Royal York Hotel with many Acton citizens in attendance. It is ironic that on the last day of its one hundredth year Beardmore was sold to Canada Packers.

During 1959 and 1960 the use of new synthetic materials as a substitute for hemlock bark forced another Canada Packers' holding firm to close its operations in Huntsville. Upwards of 50 employees and their families, from Anglo-Canadian Tanners were relocated to Acton as each department closed.

The former head office of Beardmore & Co. is still standing at 37 Front St. East, Toronto. It was sold in 1972 but the building still bears the Beardmore name.

The Beardmore tannery, which operated in Acton for over 120 years, closed its doors on September 12, 1986. ∞

ROBERT LITTLE:
OUTSTANDING EDUCATOR

A t an early age Robert Little acquired a taste for books and when only 13, in 1848 he was appointed a Junior Assistant at the Lancastrian Night School in Edinburgh, Scotland. Robert Little attended an academy as a student during the day, taught at night school and then rose at 6 a.m. to give lessons in arithmetic to a merchant, for which he received a half crown per week.

Robert Little was born February 7, 1835 at Woolwich, Kent, England. In 1850, Little was appointed first of three assistant teachers in the Sessional School of St. Andrew's Parish, Edinburgh. In April, 1852 he came to Canada with his family and upon arrival in Toronto presented a letter of introduction from his teachers in Edinburgh to the Rev. Mr. Gale, Principal of Knox College. This led to his appointment August 2, 1852 as a teacher at S.S. No. 5 Esquesing, near the Scotch Block.

In 1863, with a reputation for successful teaching, he was appointed Principal of Acton Public School. His tenure at Acton was a long and fruitful one. He gained the respect and confidence of both students and parents.

Many Acton students of a former generation could relate the outstanding teaching abilities of Robert Little or 'Old Bob Little' as some students referred to him. A nerve problem in his left arm never impaired Mr. Little's ability to 'use the rod' for any school room pranks.

It was during his supervision of the school that the many fine trees on the present Robert Little School grounds were planted. He sent students into the neigh-

FORMER STUDENTS OF ROBERT LITTLE UNVEIL A GRANITE MONUMENT IN HIS MEMORY, JULY 1900 AT ACTON CEMETERY.

ROBERT LITTLE (1835-1885)

bouring woods to bring small maple trees for planting and assigned a scholar to each tree for watering and care.

A love for one of his students resulted in the marriage of Robert Little and Sarah Johnson, the daughter of an Esquesing farmer, on May 23, 1856. They lived in Acton and eventually had a home built on Church Street. The wide halls and spacious rooms made several citizens believe that the new home would one day be the nucleus of a high school building for Acton. However, the death of Robert Little and a fire one cold January night several years later, ruined this possibility.

Little acted as the Knox Presbyterian Sunday School Superintendent for many years and although he was known as an 'old fashioned Presbyterian', he subscribed to the building fund for the new Methodist Church in Acton.

In 1871 Little was appointed Inspector of Public Schools for Halton County and also acted as Town inspector for the Board of Education for both Milton and Oakville. The chief Superintendent of Education for Ontario nominated Little as Senior Acting Inspector of Parry Sound and Algoma District in 1875.

During 1880 he helped compile *Lovell's Advanced Geography* which was used in public schools throughout Canada. In 1884 he prepared with two other educators the *New Series of Ontario School Readers*. He would not accept any remuneration for his work on the education books.

Robert Little died on April 8, 1885, after an attack of typhoid fever. He was deeply mourned by the entire community. After the funeral services a large gathering met in his old schoolroom and tributes were made by former pupils and acquaintances.

A reunion of Little's 'old pupils' was held in July, 1894 and again in July 1900. Trains brought old school mates from distant points for the unveiling of a granite monument on July 13, 1900 at Mr. Little's grave in Fairview Cemetery, Acton. Activities during the weekend reunion included a visit to the old schoolhouse, tours around the streets of Acton, a banquet at the school and an open-air concert featuring the Acton Cornet Band, with evening recitals held in the Town Hall.

Robert Little School in Acton is a monument to an educator who was held in high esteem by his pupils and who helped elevate the school standards in this province. ✖

SIR DONALD MANN: RAILROAD
BUILDER OF THE WEST

*O*ne of Canada's most remarkable men was born on *March 23, 1853 just outside Acton, on Lot 28, Concession 4, north of the old Bannockburn School. Sir Donald Mann, the fifth child of Hugh and Helen Mann, rejected his parents' plans for him to become a Presbyterian minister and went on to become one of the most colourful and enterprising men of his time.*

Of Scottish ancestry, Mann received his education in Acton. At the age of 21 he left farm life and became foreman of a lumber company in Northern Ontario. Donald, like many young Ontario men, then went west to Winnipeg, working on the railroad to seek his fortune.

By 1886, he had met William Mackenzie and established the famous contracting firm MacKenzie and Mann which in 1895 purchased the Charter of the Canadian Northern Railway. The firm eventually controlled over 8 000 kilometres of railway in the west and in northern Ontario.

Several small contracts were undertaken by the company as well as construction of the track at Crow's Nest Pass in 1897 at the then phenomenal cost of $16 500 per kilometre.

The 'King and Duke' as they were dubbed expanded their holdings by accepting financial handouts from all levels of government. They gave business to subcontractors who were frequently of their own creation. They built hotels, created telegraph companies and grain-handling companies, acquired coal and iron mines. They created trust companies and at one time, controlled the Toronto Suburban Railway which was the electric radial system from Toronto to Guelph, via Georgetown and Acton. Mann envisioned a network of these electric railways throughout southern Ontario which would feed his Canadian Northern system.

As outright gifts, The Canadian Northern had in 1913 received more than 2.8 million hectares of government land, in addition to a quarter of a billion dollars in cash and guarantees from public funds. The Laurier administration spent many a session in debate regarding the provision of further funds to MacKenzie and Mann. Two young lawyers who led the debates later became Prime Ministers. Arthur Meighen pressed the case for MacKenzie and Mann, while Richard Bennett argued that the duo wanted the country to pay their debts.

The MacKenzie and Mann Company was on the verge of bankruptcy and was eventually taken over by the federal government and incorporated into the Canadian National Railways.

When railroad construction came to an end in the west, Mann travelled to the United States contracting and eventually spent a year in South America constructing a railway for the Chilean government.

It is said that while in China trying to obtain business for the firm, Sir Donald met a Russian Count at a night club. The count took offence to a remark made by Sir Donald and challenged him to a duel with swords. Following his companion's advice, Sir Donald accepted the challenge, but insisted that the weapons be the broad-axe, as it was the national weapon of Canada! The duel did not take place!

Sir Donald married Jennie Williams at Winnipeg in March, 1887 and they had one son, Donald Cameron. He was knighted by King George V in 1911 and attended the King's Coronation in that year.

Although Sir Donald was considered to be a man of few words, he certainly was a very opinionated individual. He was the author of articles on national questions and contributed to the *National Review, Saturday Evening Post* and several other periodicals.

Although Sir Donald was a public figure for many years and became extremely wealthy and well-travelled,

SIR DONALD MANN (1853-1934).

WHEN SIR DONALD VISITED ACTON HIS PRIVATE RAILROAD CAR WOULD BE PARKED ON A SIDING NEAR THE GRAND TRUNK STATION.

THIS HOUSE LOCATED AT 284 QUEEN STREET IN ACTON WAS PURCHASED FOR HUGH MANN BY HIS SON, SIR DONALD. HUGH MANN WAS BURIED FROM THE HOME IN 1911.

he never forgot his home in Acton. His private train would pull into town onto a siding near the Acton railway station while he visited his father, who died in 1911 in Acton.

H.P. Moore, in his recollections of early Acton, recalls when Sir Donald returned to Acton and paid every cent that he owed to a group of local men from an old debt which resulted in Donald and a brother losing a farm near Crewson's Corners in their youth. A few days later the surprised creditors got together and held a fine banquet for him at the Dominion Hotel.

Sir Donald Mann died in Toronto at the age of 81 on November 10, 1934. In spite of his years, he maintained a daily contact with his business affairs and visited his office up to the very day he died. ✖

W. H. STOREY: ENTERPRISE STARTS WITH GLOVE COMPLAINT

The company became one of the major industries in Acton, employing over 200 'hands'. During the late 1800's the Canada Glove Works was reputed to be one of the largest in its class in Canada. The firm manufactured over 70 varieties of gloves and mitts, from heavy work gloves to fine wear for men and ladies.

William Hyslop Storey was born March 8, 1837 in the village of Ayton, Yorkshire, England. The only son of George and Jane Storey, he came to Canada with his parents in 1845. The Storey family made their first home on Dundas Street, near the village of Lambton, York County. It was here Storey apprenticed himself in the saddlery business.

Having completed his apprenticeship he commenced business with J. F. Taylor in Acton in 1856. The firm, known as Storey and Taylor Saddlers, was dissolved by mutual agreement in 1859. Taylor established a saddlery in Georgetown and Storey maintained the business in Acton.

Around 1868 Edward Moore, a partner in the Moore Bros. Shingle and Stave Co., visited Storey's Saddlery and complained about the poor quality gloves he had to work with and the lack of a heavy work glove on the

W. H. STOREY (1837-1898).

market. This problem was an inspiration for Storey. He borrowed a frayed pair of gloves and used them as a pattern for the coarser pair he had available within a few days. From this grew the W. H. Storey Glove Company (later known as The Canada Glove Works) established in 1868.

In 1875 the firm erected a tannery for their own glove leathers thus eliminating foreign supply and providing employment for Actonians. The only business place ever located on Bower Avenue was the Canada Glove Works, which was housed in a very attractive three-storey brick building. The first electrically-lighted sign in Acton was on the roof of the building. The sign was 30 metres long and its message would reflect in nearby Henderson's Pond "W. H. Storey & Son Glove Manufacturers, Established 1868".

Generations of Acton families worked at the Canada Glove Works. It is said that Storey had a very real concern for his employees and even when business was poor for a period of time, he would make every effort to keep on the payroll those depending on wages to maintain a household.

It was Storey who was instrumental in organizing a citizens' petition to incorporate Acton as a village in 1873. He served as the first Reeve of Acton and continued as a councillor for 18 years. In 1889 he was Warden of Halton County.

He was a Justice of the Peace for over a quarter of a century and was chairman of the school board and active in establishing Acton's Free Public Library. Storey was director of several insurance companies and served as president of the Canadian Manufacturers Association.

For over 40 years he was a member of the Methodist Church and in 1875 acted as chairman of the building committee which erected the former United Church on Mill Street near Elgin.

In 1857 Storey married Hannah Jane Smith and they raised three sons and four daughters. He died on March 6, 1898 and was buried on what would have been his 61st birthday. An indication of his esteem in the community is that over 1 000 people were unable to gain admittance to the Methodist Church for the funeral service.

Storey was succeeded by his son W. A. Storey as president of the firm. He retired in 1915 and the business was purchased by H. T. Arnold and Sons Glove Company from Georgetown. The business was carried on by the Arnolds in the Storey name until the company was dissolved in 1954. The fine brick building erected for the Storey Glove Works was razed to make way for the present Acton Post Office.

THE STOREY GLOVE WORKS BUILDING ON BOWER STREET DOMINATES THE BACKGROUND IN THIS EARLY PHOTO. STOREY'S HOME 'SUNDERVILLA' IS THE LARGE BUILDING NEAR THE CENTRE.

AN EARLY VIEW OF W. H. STOREY'S RESIDENCE KNOWN AS 'SUNDERVILLA', NOW A FUNERAL HOME AT 55 MILL STREET EAST.

Storey's residence at the corner of John and Mill Streets in Acton (55 Mill Street East and called "Sundervilla") was built in the late 1800's. It was the first home in Acton to be heated by steam, which was piped underground from the factory. In winter, the heat from the pipes created a hole on the street.

The building was taken over eventually by the Great World War Veterans Association and later served as a hotel. In 1937 Victor Rumley purchased the old mansion, which had been sitting idle since the depression, for his funeral business. Bruce E. Shoemaker purchased the business in 1953 and operated from the old Storey residence until he sold to Trillium Funeral Homes in August, 1995. ∞

SYMON FAMILY: EARLY ACTON HARDWARE MERCHANTS

It was Symon's Hardware in Acton that supplied all hardware goods for the Toronto Suburban Railway which operated through the Halton Hills area between 1917 and 1931. A purchasing agent for the Radial line enquired about a piece of railroad hardware at the Symon store when the line was being surveyed. He was amazed to find that James Symon not only had access to the item but was also familiar with railroad jargon and knew the functions of hardware unique to the railroad industry.

Charles and James Symon, natives of Scotland, were forerunners of a long tradition of Symons in the business history of Acton.

Charles was a lumberman and held the contract to supply railroad ties for the Toronto-Guelph Railway (later purchased by the Grand Trunk). Acton was at one time the centre of a large lumbering business and during the 1860's Charles and brother Jimmie operated a grocery store which stood at the site of the present Bank of Montreal at Mill and Willow Streets. In 1872, the business was sold to Messrs. D.D. Christie and David Henderson of Milton. Charles Symon and family relocated to Parry Sound, where he acted as manager of the new Guelph Lumber Company.

Charles died at Parry Sound in 1879 and at the age of 14 the eldest son, James, assumed responsibility for the household with his mother. Mrs. Symon (1842-1910) and family returned to the Acton area in the early 1880's. She was formerly Helen Brown Allan and it was at the Allan farm on the Second Concession, Esquesing directly above Acton that the mother and children lived.

The new generation of Symon brothers attempted several business ventures in the area, including an onion crop on the Quantis farm (on Queen Street East at Acton Blvd.). The Symon Brothers' grocery store prospered downtown for many years. An issue of the *Acton Free Press* dated February 1897 dubs the enterprise a "Cheap Cash Store" and announces that effective March 1st "business will be strictly cash". A barrel of choice apples was given to any purchaser of $10 worth of goods paid in cash within the month. Alec Symon and brother-in-law Robert Campbell were partners in a jewellery business on Mill Street.

The eldest son James (1864-1935) married Elizabeth MacPherson (1874-1957) on the MacPherson farm once owned by Beardmore and Company. The newlyweds moved to Guelph for a number of years where James was a 'traveller' or sales representative for two Kitchener glove manufacturers.

In 1905 this branch of the Symon family moved back to Acton and James purchased the hardware business

JAMES SYMON INSIDE THE SYMON HARDWARE STORE, 22 MILL STREET EAST.

DON'T GRUMBLE

About poorly cooked meals ; buy a

Duchess of Oxford

And you'll have no further cause of complaint. In this range the fire is so easily regulated—answering to a touch ; and the oven so easily ventilated and heated uniformly throughout, that even a poor cook can't help being successful in preparing the daintiest dishes.

FOR SALE BY SYMON BROS, ACTON.
The Gurney Foundry Co., Ltd Toronto.

A SYMON BROS. ADVERTISEMENT, *ACTON FREE PRESS*, JULY 2, 1896.

MAC SYMON AND ROD RYDER POSE AT SYMON'S HARDWARE, 43 MILL STREET EAST IN THE 1940'S.

of Reg Johnstone. Reg was the son of William Johnstone, the undertaker in Acton for many years.

Thirty Willow Street was built for James Symon in 1915. A family story relates that a stove was sold from the house to the construction crew of the Radial line. Apparently at the time of the sale the stove was still burning wood and Mrs. Symon had to rescue some baking from the oven while it was being carried out the door!

Symon Hardware was later relocated down Mill Street and shortly after James' death in 1935 Mrs. Symon arranged for the erection of the brick building at 43 Mill Street East. It was on this site that Acton's first movie house was built by William Johnstone and operated by Morris Saxe and later H. S. Holmes. James' son 'Mac' Symon and daughter Marguerite worked for their mother in the hardware business until her death in 1957, and eventually 'Mac' assumed control of the business. Symon Hardware was sold in 1972 to Mike Kinal who now operates Acton Home Hardware on the same premises. ⚒

Limehouse Historical Overview

Limehouse is situated on the main Canadian National Railway line approximately 56 kilometres west of Toronto. It is between Acton and Georgetown, approximately 5 kilometres from each at the intersection of Concession 5 and Regional Road 43. Black Creek winds through the village.

It was 1820 when Adam Stull obtained the Crown Deed for Lot 22, Concession 6, Esquesing Township. Approximately two years later John Meredith took possession of neighbouring Lot 23. In 1840 a Mr Clendenning purchased both properties and carried on a saw mill operation, naming the community Fountain Green.

Although many pioneer farmers burned lime locally on their farms in a very primitive manner, the lime industry got its start in the area commercially in the early 1840's when Lindsay and Farquhar opened their 'set' lime kilns.

The Niagara Escarpment, which snakes through Halton, was both an obstacle for transportation and a provider of raw material for the early settler. Bescoby and Worthington had established yet another lime kiln operation in the area by the early 1850's. In 1857 Gowdy and Moore purchased the Bescoby works and operated the entire lime business in the community under the Toronto Lime Company for nearly 60 years.

The two types of lime kilns used in the Gowdy and Moore operation were known as 'set' and 'draw' kilns. The set was approximately 3 metres high and dated back to the 1840's. Firewood was placed in the kiln from the top with limestone and necessary ingredients. The kiln would burn for five to six days with wood continuously being added in the fire holes at the bottom front of the kiln. Lime chunks (about the size of cement blocks) would then be removed out of the fire hole. Set kilns were not very efficient as a charge had to be placed, burned and then shut down while cooling before the operation could be repeated.

The 'draw' kilns were much taller (approximately 16 metres) and were introduced in the 1870's. Although

THE LIMEHOUSE STORE AND HOTEL ABOUT 1905.

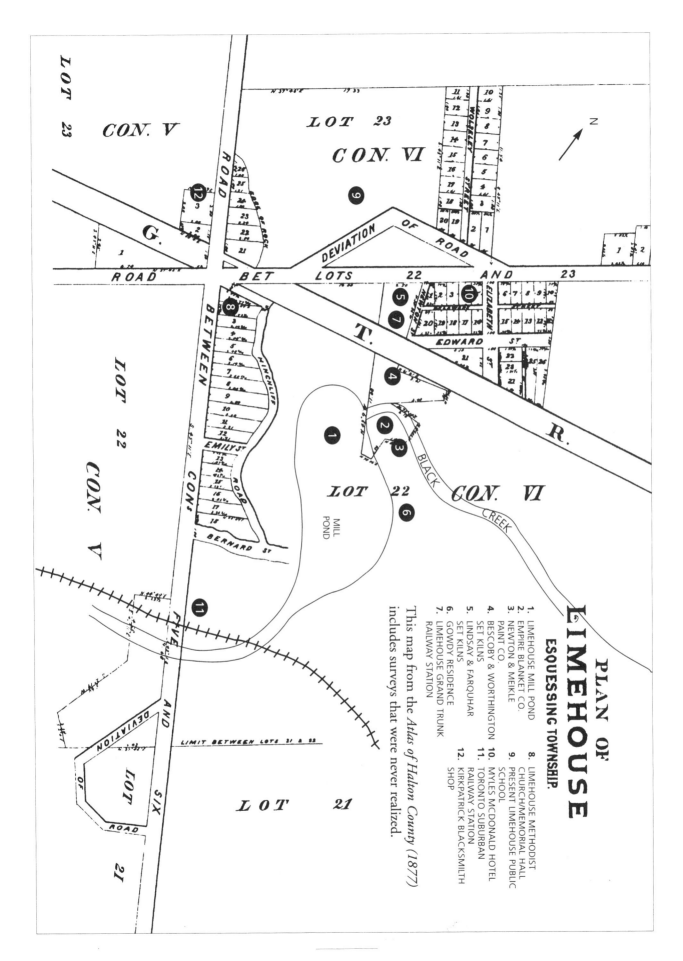

PLAN OF
LIMEHOUSE

ESQUESSING TOWNSHIP.

1. LIMEHOUSE MILL POND
2. EMPIRE BLANKET CO.
3. NEWTON & MEIKLE
   PAINT CO.
4. BESCOBY & WORTHINGTON
   SET KILNS
5. LINDSAY & FARQUHAR
   SET KILNS
6. GOWDY RESIDENCE
7. LIMEHOUSE GRAND TRUNK
   RAILWAY STATION

8. LIMEHOUSE METHODIST
   CHURCH/MEMORIAL HALL
9. PRESENT LIMEHOUSE PUBLIC
   SCHOOL
10. MYLES MCDONALD HOTEL
11. TORONTO SUBURBAN
    RAILWAY STATION
12. KIRKPATRICK BLACKSMITH
    SHOP

This map from the *Atlas of Halton County* (1877)
includes surveys that were never realized.

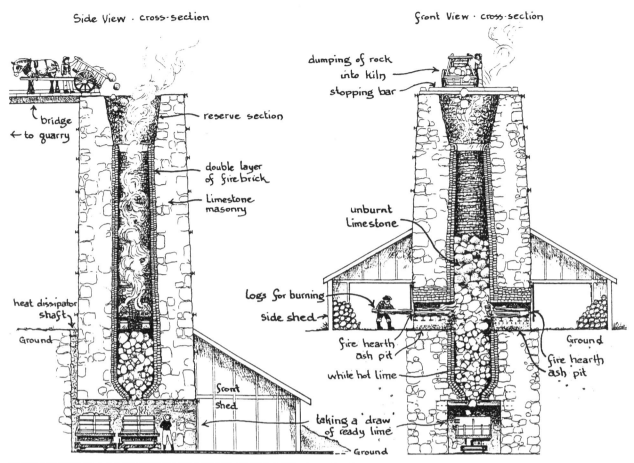

Side View · cross-section

bridge
← to quarry

reserve section

double layer
of firebrick

Limestone
masonry

heat dissipator
shaft

Ground

Front
shed

Front View · cross-section

dumping of rock
into kiln

stopping bar

unburnt
limestone

logs for burning

side shed

fire hearth
ash pit

white hot lime

taking a 'draw'
of ready lime

Ground

fire hearth
ash pit

Ground

CROSS-SECTIONS OF A 'DRAW' KILN (HALTON REGION CONSERVATION AUTHORITY).

the draw kilns required a three-day startup period they could be operated around the clock with no shut down required. The walls were braced from top to bottom to prevent bulging of the limestone exterior due to the extreme heat. With the draw kiln system lime could be drawn out through fire boxes on three sides of the kiln every five or six hours. The top of the kiln was level with the floor of the quarry and a ramp would carry a horse and wagon load of raw materials to the opening at the top.

The lime industry closed in the area around 1915 because the blasting and quarrying operation was continually moving closer to the residential area. A serious injury did occur in 1915 and a law suit was filed. The set and draw kilns were also becoming outdated and larger manufacturers were buying out smaller competitors. This was the case when the Toronto Lime Works property was purchased by Gypsum Lime and Alabaster in 1927.

John Newton left England for the new world in 1842 and settled in Fountain Green, where he established a successful woollen manufacturing business. He had worked in the wool-combing trade since his youth in both England and Ireland. By 1850 Newton had built a mill on Black Creek for the production of cement. It was Newton's company that provided cement for the bridges and other works during the building of the Grand Trunk Railway through the area. By 1862 Newton had opened yet another business known as the Empire Blanket Company.

Ten years later Newton and a partner named Meikle started a fireproof paint company, which was taken over by Newton's son James in 1874. His other sons, John and Isaac, were also active in various aspects of the business. The paint company sold to Canada, the United States, Britain and Australia and won a number of prizes, including a bronze medal at the Chicago World's Fair in 1896.

Newton became a Justice of the Peace for the area and changed the name of the community from Fountain Green to Limehouse when he became the first postmaster in 1857.

Although Limehouse was a bustling industrial concern from the 1850's it was still relatively slow to grow compared with surrounding communities. The village wasn't surveyed until 1856 and by 1861 there were only 17 registered landowners in the village.

A REAR VIEW OF THE COMMERCIAL DISTRICT IN LIMEHOUSE TAKEN FROM THE GRAND TRUNK STATION.

The Halton County Atlas in 1877 shows a larger survey which never developed.

The building of the railway through the village during the early 1850's brought some prosperity, along with fights at local hotels while the railway building crews passed through the area. Considerable time was spent in Limehouse for the cutting and blasting required to put the line through the rocky terrain. The decision to build the Grand Trunk Railroad through Limehouse certainly encouraged the shipment of large quantities of lumber, lime, paint and other products: *The Halton County Atlas* recorded over 4 000 tons of freight being shipped from Limehouse Station as early as 1876. Eventually four passenger trains stopped daily, while freight trains called at least twice a week.

Telephone service was introduced to Limehouse in 1885. There was only one subscriber that year: "The Toronto Lime Company, John Moore, Manager, Limeworks". Limehouse was originally under the Acton exchange, but in 1901 a telephone station was established at the Toronto Lime Company for all residents. The service became the responsibility of the Georgetown telephone agent by 1913.

On October 12, 1893 the entire village was threatened by a fire which completely destroyed the woollen, paint and lumber mills including 100 cords of wood stored to fire the kilns of the Toronto Lime Company. The Georgetown Fire Brigade saved the day—and the village! Newton, however did not carry adequate insurance coverage to rebuild.

The first school in Limehouse area was a log structure probably built in the mid-1840's. Its movement around the community has been well documented and later the structure was relocated to Churchill (north of Acton) to be used as a hog pen. In 1862 the first floor of the old stone school—known as SS No. 9 or 'Gibraltar'—was built with a second storey added in 1875. The building is situated south of the village on the Fifth Line. In later years the upstairs was not used, probably due to the decline in manufacturing after the 1893 fire and the eventual closing of the lime works. By 1954, however, the school population had increased to the point that the upstairs was reopened at no cost to the taxpayers due to the hard work from volunteers in the community, particularly Mr. and Mrs. Fred Brooks. The additional demand had nothing to do with new industry in the area, but was a consequence of the baby boom after World War Two, with commuters working in places like Acton, Georgetown, Brampton and Malton. The old school closed its doors in June 1962 and the new Limehouse school opened in September of that year. The new school building is situated in the centre of the village.

THE 1913 CLASS OF GIBRALTAR SCHOOL POSE BEFORE THE SCHOOL, WHICH OPENED IN 1862 AND CLOSED ITS DOORS ONE HUNDRED YEARS LATER.

THOMAS GOWDY DEEDED THE LAND FOR THE LIMEHOUSE METHODIST CHURCH IN 1876. IN 1945 IT BECAME A COMMUNITY HALL THANKS TO THE EFFORTS OF THE LIMEHOUSE WOMEN'S INSTITUTE.

RELATIVES OF THE AUTHOR AT THE LIMEHOUSE 'RADIAL' STATION (STOP 77) ON THE FIFTH LINE. AUNT MARGARET (REAR), UNCLE HECTOR, COUSIN JEAN AND UNCLE NORMAN MCDONALD.

The station was a convenient walk down the Fifth Line across from the Mitchell property just south of the village.

There are two buildings in Limehouse associated with worship. Land for a cemetery and church was deeded in 1832 by John Meredith to the trustees of the Presbyterian Church on the Sixth Line. In 1858 Myles McDonald, a local hotelkeeper and carpenter, commenced work on the church building, which opened in October 1861. The local Anglicans and the Methodists also supported the Presbyterian Church and consequently were given the right to hold services in the church. The other building is on land deeded to the Methodists of the area in 1876 by Thomas Gowdy. The stone church was closed after church union and purchased by the Limehouse Women's Institute in 1945 for a community hall in honour of area men and women who fought in the World Wars.

At one time before the bridge was built, the Fifth Line crossed the Grand Trunk Railroad in the village at a level crossing immediately west of the present village and north of the Limehouse Memorial Hall. This portion of the Fifth Line was known as Maple Avenue. By late 1982 the Region of Halton and Canadian National Railways made investigations about the load-carrying capacity of the Limehouse bridge. As a result, the load limit was reduced from 10 tonnes to 5 tonnes in January 1983. By that November, the CN work crews had rehabilitated the structure by replacing deteriorated steel supports and timber deck. An asphalt riding surface was also introduced to preserve the new timber.

The once bustling village of Limehouse which had three hotels, two quarries, blanket, paint and cement manufacturers, saw and woollen mills, blacksmiths and three stores at one time is now a quiet community from which its residents commute to neighbouring towns. The area is now known for its natural beauty, particularly evident when one walks the nearby Bruce Trail. Remnants of some of the bustling businesses established by people like Gowdy, Moore and Newton attract the historian. ◈

Limehouse had its own 'stop' on the Toronto Suburban Radial Line between 1917 and 1931. The line ran immediately south of the village and crossed the mill pond with a curved wooden trestle. Although the Toronto Suburban Railway line was not built through the centre of the village it was close to the lime works.

GOWDYS OF LIMEHOUSE

For over 37 years the William Gowdy family lived in Limehouse. There wasn't an aspect of the community in which the Gowdys didn't give a helping hand. Much of the time Limehouse was a bustling village with teams of horses bringing wood to fire the kilns and wagon loads of supplies for the many industries located along Black Creek which winds through the village.

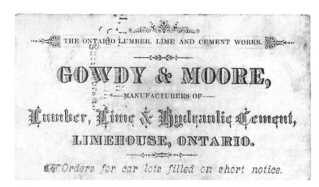

GOWDY & MOORE BUSINESS CARD.

The lime kilns built and originally owned by Messrs. Bescoby and Worthington were located in Limehouse just south of the Grand Trunk railway line. Their ruins still stand as a monument to the past industry.

In 1857 Messrs. T. Gowdy and his brother-in-law J. Moore purchased the Bescoby works. Thomas Gowdy was born in Toronto on October 10, 1831 and moved to Guelph in his youth. Very ambitious at an early age, Thomas served his apprenticeship as a plasterer before entering into partnership with John Stewart at Guelph. He later became a prominent manufacturer of farm implements for over 14 years in Guelph, where he also served as alderman for a number of years and was elected mayor in 1889 and 1890.

Gowdy was a director of several well-established insurance companies including Dominion Life. He was an original director of the Guelph Junction Railroad as well as a director of the Guelph General Hospital. He was president of the Gowdy-Moore Lime Company until his death on December 3, 1913. (A partnership had been entered with Moore, who had previously been engaged in the lumber and shingle business.)

Thomas Gowdy married Margaret Moore in Acton on May 3, 1864. Miss Moore was an aunt to H. P. Moore, a former editor and publisher of *The Acton Free Press*. Mrs. Gowdy died in Guelph on March 7, 1925.

It was Thomas Gowdy who, in 1876, deeded the land for the Limehouse Methodist Church which was eventually closed after the church union of 1925. In 1945 it was bought by the Limehouse Women's Institute for a community hall in memory of local people who fought in the two world wars.

WORKERS POSE AT THE GOWDY & MOORE LIME WORKS AT LIMEHOUSE.

A VIEW OF THE MILL POND AND INDUSTRIAL SITE FROM LIMEHOUSE VILLAGE. A DRAW KILN IS BURNING NEAR THE CENTRE OF THE PHOTOGRAPH.

William Newton Douglas Gowdy (Thomas' fourth son) was born at Guelph on November 26, 1870 and married Mary Holmes from Nassagaweya on August 24, 1898. His venture into business started in the grocery trade at Guelph and after a few years he became the manager of Standard White Lime company at Beachville, Ontario.

William became a manager of the Toronto Lime Company at Limehouse in 1906 upon the retirement of his uncle John Moore. He continued as manager of the Limehouse and nearby Dolly Varden plants until they were taken over by Gypsum Lime and Alabastine Co.

William Gowdy was a Justice of the Peace and served as a Deputy Reeve and Reeve of Esquesing Township during the 1920's. He was a member of the school board for the old S.S. No. 9 or Gibraltar School which still stands just below the village on the Fifth Concession and is now a private home. William had a musical talent, as he was superintendent of Sunday School choirs and performed as soloist at various local events.

Due to the concentration of manufacturing facilities the Limehouse kiln operations were eventually closed down. The last burning of the kilns was about 1915. In its peak period during the 1880's the lime works of Gowdy and Moore employed over 100 men on a three-shift basis and produced over 75 000 bushels of lime a year from the six kilns.

The Gowdy-Moore sawmill had a capacity of over 3 000 metres of lumber a day. The account of goods shipped from the Limehouse Station during 1876 was 4 130 tons, principally lime and lumber at a cost of over $5 000.

With the closing of the Limehouse facilities, William Gowdy retired and moved to Acton in 1943 until his death on August 24, 1948. After the death of his first wife, he married Mary Hoppman of Detroit on August 18, 1927. She is well remembered for her love of music and formed a music club in Acton during the 1950's. She was also an active member of the Limehouse Women's Institute.

William Gowdy's son Douglas, who was born in 1899, was a well-respected member of the community and through his career held various managerial positions with *The Financial Post* and MacLean-Hunter Publications.

In 1942 William Gowdy sold the property, which had once been the location of lime kilns and various mills, to a Mr. G. France of Toledo, Ohio, who had some interest in the lime and quarrying business. No developments resulted.

On January 16, 1967 the Credit Valley Conservation Authority purchased over 35 hectares, including the former Gowdy property. It has been the intention of the Authority to restore the kilns as nearly as possible to the original. One of the first undertakings was to demolish the empty Gowdy home which had been vandalised. The Authority has developed plans for the area but is restricted by budgets.

One remnant of the Gowdys is preserved for posterity: the old three-seater outhouse from the Gowdy farm is now on display at Black Creek Pioneer Village in Toronto. ⚭

SID KIRKPATRICK: THE LAST LIMEHOUSE BLACKSMITH

Although a blacksmith by trade, Sid (as he was known by all) could turn his hand to many odd jobs. He was always ready to attend to the repairs at the homes of neighbours and friends after his own day's work was done. The Kirkpatrick Blacksmith Shop in Limehouse was one of the last to close in the area.

The blacksmith was one of the most sought-after tradesmen during the early development of north Halton. Working beside a hot forge all day, these men not only made and fitted horseshoes, they manufactured and mended tools and equipment used on the farms and in local businesses.

When Robert Ford established the first blacksmith shop at Limehouse in 1857 the settlement still had hopes for growth. A post office had just been established, Gowdy & Moore were expanding the lime industry and the Grand Trunk Railway had just been built through the village with a station near the Fifth Line crossing at the lime kilns.

Ford purchased a part of Lot 23, Concession Five, Esquesing and opened his shop in the village immediately north of the railroad crossing on the Fifth Line.

The increase in business activity in the area fully required a skilled blacksmith and Ford remained in Limehouse for over 25 years. He died in Lambton County in 1901.

According to Halton land registry records the property containing the blacksmith shop was sold to Peter Mallaby in 1878 and two years later to William Hogg. Andrew Dobbie purchased the blacksmith business in 1894. Very little is known about Dobbie except that he operated the shop until the early 1920's. *The Acton Free Press* in June 1910 reported that Andrew's twenty-year-old son, Thomas, was struck and killed by a train while working near Paris, Ontario. Tom Dobbie had also worked at the Acton Grand Trunk Station.

Sid Kirkpatrick was the next blacksmith at the Limehouse shop. He was born Sidney Moffat in England in 1891 and had immigrated to Canada as a 'home boy'. He was one of some 80 000 children who arrived in this country from the British Isles between 1870 and 1930 hoping for a better life working on Canadian farms. A number of these children were placed on farms in Halton. Some were already destitute before leaving Britain only to meet with continuing hardship and loneliness when they arrived.

Sid Moffat was one of the fortunate young immigrants. He was adopted by a loving couple, Charles and Phoebe Kirkpatrick, in Limehouse. Charles, born in

SID KIRKPATRICK WITH A CUSTOMER AT THE LIMEHOUSE BLACKSMITH SHOP.

1827 in Country Antrim, Ireland, married Phoebe Dobbie in 1856. She was the daughter of Elizabeth and Andrew Dobbie of Lot 21, Concession Four, Esquesing. *The Halton Gazetteer of 1864* lists Charles Kirkpatrick as a labourer in Limehouse. He died in December 1908 on his eighty-first birthday. His widow and Sid continued to live in the Kirkpatrick home, a brick house in the centre of the village, which later served as Joe Scott's store from the early 1920's to 1959.

When Sid took over the Limehouse blacksmith shop he had already served his apprenticeship at the O'Neill Carriage Works in Georgetown. This firm operated at the corner of Main and Wesleyan Streets and was originally the Culp and Mackenzie Blacksmith and Carriage Works dating back to the 1860's.

Sid also worked in the Stewarttown area. It was here that he met Caroline Standish (1901-1978). She was a descendent of Joseph Standish (1770-1868) who had arrived in Upper Canada from Ireland in 1818 and settled on Lot 13, Concession Six, Esquesing. It was at his large and centrally located home that the first official meeting of the Township was held on New Year's Day 1821.

Sid and Caroline were married at the Standish homestead on October 31, 1923 and lived in the greystone building next to the blacksmith shop at Limehouse. Phoebe Kirkpatrick lived with them until her death in January 1929 at age 93. A right registered on the deed to the property granted a 'life estate' to Phoebe, recognizing she could live in the Limehouse home for the duration of her natural life.

The Kirkpatricks lived in Limehouse all their married life and had six children. A son, Charles, died in infancy in 1936. The Kirkpatrick home hosted many community events, including euchres and dances to raise funds for filling Christmas boxes for local men and women overseas during World War Two.

The Kirkpatrick blacksmith shop was a busy place with pieces of equipment and parts being made, but the seeding and harvesting seasons were particularly hectic with farmers relying on Sid's expertise at his forge to get them back into the field to continue their work. When he wasn't busy at the shop, he could be found in the garden working with Caroline.

Although Sid retired from the blacksmith business in 1949 he was always available to repair some piece of equipment for a neighbour. He donated most of the blacksmith equipment to the Halton Regional Museum. Sid also worked at Provincial Papers (formerly The Barber Coated Paper Mills) in Georgetown until 1956 and was caretaker of Limehouse Public school until 1968.

When Jack Noble, a local Limehouse boy, started his own car repair business in the village in the early 1950's, Sid Kirkpatrick offered his former blacksmith shop as a suitable location. Noble, who had apprenticed at Speight's Garage on Guelph Street in Georgetown, operated at the Kirkpatrick location from 1950 until he opened a new garage in 1963 immediately north of the blacksmith shop.

The Kirkpatricks were active members of Limehouse Presbyterian Church. Sid was on the Board of Managers for many years, while Caroline was a member of the Women's Missionary Society and the Limehouse Women's Institute. Their home was often the place where school teachers boarded. Glenda Benton, who arrived in the village to teach in 1956, recalls being pleased to find that Sid had built a bookcase for her. For many years she received special occasion cards from the Kirkpatricks always signed "mom and dad".

Sidney died at Limehouse on October 19, 1969. He requested that he be buried from his beloved home (as was infant son Charles in 1936). Caroline sold the property with the blacksmith shop in 1973 and died in Durham, Ontario on May 30, 1978. The street on which the property is situated is now called Kirkpatrick Lane. ∞

THE KIRKPATRICK FAMILY, LIMEHOUSE, JUNE, 1928. (L-R) SID, JAMES, PHOEBE, CAROLINE AND BABY MARY

DOLLY VARDEN: THE FASCINATION OF A NAME

A life-long fascination with the name Dolly Varden prompted my interest in the history of the area and resulted in this book. Stories have been handed down by generations of residents of Dolly Varden. One relates that a woman by that name lived there in a hut. One old-timer recalled his father, once an employee at 'The Dolly', tell the story about this mysterious woman setting fire to herself with kerosene oil.

My grandfather, Angus McDonald, purchased 40 hectares at Lot 24, Concession 4, Esquesing in 1923 and my father, Russell, grew up there with eight brothers and two sisters. I moved with my parents in 1953 to this area, called 'Dolly Varden'. The name intrigued me as a young boy. Some family members would indicate that 'The Dolly' was named after a famous opera or vaudeville star or possibly the woman referred to above.

These details were too scanty and I felt a compulsion to find out more. A letter to the British Music Hall Society in England requesting information on one Dolly Varden netted only an assumption that "she was only a character of fiction". No trace of a real-life 'Dolly Varden' on file!

Charles Dickens' novel *Barnaby Rudge,* which first appeared as a series of articles in 1841, included a principal character called Dolly Varden, "a buxom young girl…not likely frightened".

One theory is that Dickens was portraying a type of person in the Limehouse district of London. Some early immigrants settling in the present Limehouse, Ontario area would have considered her somewhat a folk hero, hence the name Dolly Varden for the small industrial community just west of Limehouse on the Grand Trunk Line.

Although the Ontario Geographic Names Board does not acknowledge the name, Dolly Varden is listed as 'Stop 80' on a Toronto Suburban Railroad schedule dated May 10, 1918. This is one of the few times Dolly Varden was ever in print as a geographic location.

'The Dolly' lay between the Third and Fourth Concessions of Esquesing Township on Lot 24, along the Grand Trunk Railroad line. The Niagara Escarpment runs through this area with beds of limestone used since the middle 1840's for making cement and plaster. Lime kilns were built at Dolly Varden by Messrs.

FOUR KILNS WERE ERECTED AT THE DOLLY VARDEN WORKS TO PRODUCE INGREDIENTS FOR CEMENT AND PLASTER.

WORKERS POSE AT THE TORONTO LIME WORKS AT DOLLY VARDEN IN 1913. 'THE DOLLY' PROVIDED EMPLOYMENT FOR SEVERAL MEN FROM THE 1870'S UNTIL 1931. AREA FARMERS SOLD WOOD TO THE FIRM FOR FIRING THE KILNS. WILLIAM GOWDY APPEARS, CENTRE, WITH THE WHITE HAT.

RAILROAD SIDINGS, LIME CARTS AND WORKERS' HOMES CAN BE SEEN IN THIS 1920'S VIEW AT DOLLY VARDEN.

Robertson and Laidlaw in 1872. Local farmers supplied the limeworks with wood for the kilns. It was not uncommon to see several loaded wagons headed for 'The Dolly'.

On May 12, 1874 Dr. McGarvin and C. S. Smith of Acton purchased the limeworks. By this time four kilns were in operation, eight months of the year, with a capacity of 1 000 bushels per day. There were about 10 men employed with total wages amounting to $325 per month.

The operation grew and eventually its name was changed from the Canada Lime Works to the Toronto Lime Company. By 1917 the dangers of blasting and a shortage of limestone resulted in closure of the Limehouse quarries. This meant a heavier concentration of activities at Dolly Varden until 1931, when the kilns were last fired.

About 10 houses once sat near the Fourth Concession immediately east of the lime kilns and were homes for workers at the kilns. According to *The Acton Free Press*, in 1920 the Toronto Lime Company was making preparations for the erection of two additional houses near the works. A barn on the property was also being converted into a dwelling.

The area sat idle until the Acton Limestone Quarries commenced operation in 1962. This became one of the largest and most modern aggregate operations in North America. In 1967 Indusmin acquired the huge Acton Limestone Quarry site which still operates today and is known as United Aggregates. ∞

Bagnell, Kenneth — *The Little Immigrants*, Toronto: Macmillan of Canada, 1980

Berton, Pierre — *Niagara*, Toronto: McClelland & Stewart, 1992

Burlington Centennial Committee — *From Pathway to Skyway: A History of Burlington*, Burlington: 1967

Carruthers, G. — *Paper in the Making*, Toronto: Garden City Press, 1947

Clarke, G. P. — *Halton's Pages of the Past*, Acton: Dills, 1955

Cook, William E. — *Milton: Welcome to Our Town*, Boston Mills: Boston Mills Press, 1977

Credit Valley Conservation Authority Report, 1957

Davis, N. F. — *The Irishman in Canada*, Shannon: Irish University Press, 1968 (Reprint of 1877 edition)

Due, J. F. — *The Inter-city Electric Railway Industry in Canada*, Toronto: University of Toronto Press, 1966

First Century of Christian Fellowship, Georgetown Baptist Church, 1947

Hewitt, D. F. and Voss, M. A. — *The Limestone Industry of Ontario*, Toronto: Ontario Ministry of Natural Resources, 1972

Houston, Richard — *Numbering the Survivors*, Toronto: Generation Press, 1979

Knox Presbyterian Church (Georgetown), 1960

Limehouse Presbyterian Church Centennial, 1961

Mathews, H. C. — *Oakville and The Sixteen*, Toronto: University of Toronto Press, 1953

Moore, H. P. and Dills, G. A. — *Acton's Early Days*, Acton: Dills Printing and Publishing, 1939

Pope, J. H. — *Historical Atlas of Halton County*, Toronto: Walker & Miles, 1877 (Stratford, Ontario: Cummings, 1977 Reprint)

Rowe, John Mark Benbow — *Glen Williams on the Credit River*, Glen Williams: St. Albans Church and Esquesing Historical Society, 1993

Rowe, John Mark Benbow — *The Story of Georgetown, Ontario*, Georgetown: Esquesing Historical Society, 1992

Rubio, Mary and Waterston, Elizabeth — *The Selected Journals of L. M. Montgomery, Volume III 1921-1929*, Toronto: Oxford University Press, 1992

Rubio, Mary and Waterston, Elizabeth — *Writing A Life*, Toronto: ECW Press, 1995

Ruggle, Rev. Richard — *Down In The Glen*, Glen Williams: Glen Williams Cemetery Board, 1978

Ruggle, Rev. Richard — *Norval on the Credit*, Erin, Ontario: Press Porcepic, 1973

Salmon, J. V. — *Rails from the Junction*, Toronto: 1969

Smith, W. L. — *Pioneers of Old Ontario*, Toronto: Morang, 1923

St. George's Anglican Church Centennial (Georgetown, 1952

Various issues of *The Acton Free Press, The Georgetown Herald, The Georgetown Independent, The Canadian Champion*

Archival and Special Collections, Montgomery Collection, University of Guelph Library

Halton Region Conservation Authority Collection

Eaton's of Canada Archives, picture collection

'Anne of Green Gables' and 'Green Gables House' are trademarks and Canadian Official Marks of the Anne of Green Gables Licensing Authority, which is owned by the Heirs of L.M. Montgomery and the Province of Prince Edward Island and located in Charlottetown, Prince Edward Island.

INDEX

Limehouse Public School 113, 114, 119
Limehouse Women's Institute 114, 115, 116, 119
Lindsay & Farquahar Limeworks 110
Little, Robert family 96, 102-103
Lorne Scots 35, 45, 50, 86
Lyons, Slick 75

M
Macdonald, Rev. Ewan family 83, 90-93
MacIntosh, Dr. A. 33
Mackenzie & Mann 104-105
Mackenzie, J. B. family 6, 22, 25, 27, 36, 42-43, 62, 63, 64, 72, 82
Mackenzie, William 104
Mackenzie, William Lyon 12
MacPherson, Elizabeth 108
Mallaby, Peter 118
Mann, Sir Donald family 60, 97, 104-105
Markou, George and Nick 53
Martin, Marie 37
Mason, Amos 97
Mason Knitting 97, 98
McCallum, H. A. 22
McCallum's Grist Mill 94
McClure, Sam 93
McDonald, Angus family 35, 115, 120
McGarvin, Dr. 121
McGarvin, J. 96
McGibbon Hotel 24, 31, 46, 51-53, 57, 60
McGibbon, Sam family 51-53
McGilvray, Garfield 20
McGloshen & Atcheson 99
McLaughlan Group 9, 66
McNab, James 80, 84
McNab, Mary Margaret 48
McNabville 48, 80-83, 84
McNally Construction 45
McQueen, Eliza 42
Mechanics Institute 14
Melrose Knitting Co. 70
Meredith, John 110, 115
Metropolitan Bank 85
Milton Inn 51
Mitchell, Colonel 80, 84
Moffat, Sidney 118
Montgomery, Lucy Maud family 82, 90-93
Moore Bros. Shingle and Stove Co. 106
Moore Park 8

Moore, Edward 106
Moore, H. P. 62, 94, 105, 116
Moore, John 74
Moore, Joseph family 62-63
Moore, Margaret 116
Morton's Barber Shop 54
Muirhead, John Butler 68
Murray, Colonel 34

N
Nelles, Abraham 94, 99
Nellis, Cecil 98
Newton, John 112
Niagara Escarpment 2, 110, 120
Nipigon Pulp & Paper Co. 14
Noble, Irwin 61
Noble, Jack 119
Noble, Robert family 80, 84-86
Noble's Flour Mill 60, 84-86
North Halton Golf & Country Club 9, 23, 36, 41, 47
Norval 2, 29, 60, 76, 80-83
Norval Presbyterian Church 29 83, 86, 90-93
Norval Railroad Station 80, 82, 84, 87

O
O'Neill Carriage Works 8, 46, 119
Olde Hide House 98
Ontario Electrical Railway Historical Assoc. 61
Oxford Picture Frame Co. 38

P
Patrick, Hannah 14
Penrice, Sam family 70, 77
Perron of Montreal 45
Phillips, Colonel 41
Ponds of Georgetown 18-19, 52
Porter, H. K. 98
Prohibition 52, 57
Prospect Park 96
Provincial Paper Co. 9, 14, 36, 119

R
Railroad Exchange Hotel 56-57
Reed, Julian and Marion 86
Reid, Luella 92
Reid, Robert family 20, 28-30, 92
Reynold's Paint Factory 18
Robertson & Laidlaw 121
Roche, Mazo de la 97
Rosse, George 76
Roxy Theatre 42

Royal Canadian Legion, Acton 98, 101
Royal Canadian Legion, Georgetown 6, 8, 22, 35, 42
Rubio, Mary 93
Ruggle, Richard Rev. 68
Rumley, Victor 107

S
Sacré Coeur Church 47
Saxe, Morris family 38-39, 109
Saxifrage 49
Scotch Block 1, 51, 80, 102
Scott, Jennie 87
Scott, Ray 60
Secord, Sarah Augusta 96, 97
Set kiln 110, 112
Seynuck Farm 97
Shepherd, John family 34-35
Shoemaker, Bruce 107
Sid-Mac building 19
Silver Creek 6, 13, 16, 18, 24, 32, 33, 46, 49, 60
Simcoe, John Graves 34
Smith & Stone Ltd. 6, 24, 40-41
Smith, Bill 55
Smith, C. S. 121
Smith, Hannah Jane 106
Smith, William family 6, 40-41
Snyder, Mildred 37
Speight, Arthur 55
Speight Garage 119
Speight, Thomas 26
St. Alban's Anglican Church 73
St. George's Anglican Church 10, 11, 18, 19, 35, 38, 60, 77
St. John's United Church 50, 64
St. Paul's Anglican Church 87
St. Paul's Parish Hall 91, 92
St. Stephen's Anglican Church 59
Standish, Joseph and Caroline 119
Stewart, John 116
Stewarttown 2, 4, 20, 24, 34, 35, 52
Stone, Benny family 6, 40-41
Storey & Taylor Saddlers 106
Storey Glove Works 106-107
Storey, W. H. family 26, 94, 106-107
Stull, Adam 110
Sundervilla 107
Swan, Robert 94
Sykes and Ainsley Mill 70
Sykes, Hattie 54
Symon Hardware 108, 109
Symon, James family 108-109

T
Taylor, J. F. 106
Thompson, Elmer 14
Thompson, Ray 88
Toronto Lime Co. 110, 112, 113
Toronto Suburban Railway ('Radial') 8, 9, 18, 23, 27, 32, 60-61, 82, 84, 87, 97, 104, 108, 109, 115, 120
Tost, Jack 11
Tost, Nan 75
Townsend, Elwin 93
Trafalgar Road 2, 58
Tyers, Edward 61

U
Underground Railroad 34
Union Presbyterian Church 29, 90-93
United Aggregates 121
University Avenue Synagogue 31
Upper Canada College 82, 85

V
Victoria Electric Supply Co. 40
Viejalinen, Luella 93

W
Wallace, Brigadier 41
Warren, R. D. 62
Watchtower Bible & Tract Society 32
Webb family 91, 92
Webster, Dr. Samuel 15, 82
Wheeler, John A. family 72, 74-75, 88
Wilber Lake 13
Wildwood 10, 11, 32
Williams Mill & Creative Arts School 24, 72
Williams, Benajah family 18, 68-73, 74
Williams, Jennie 104
Williamsburg 68-73
Willoughby, John A. family 6, 8, 22-23, 35, 36, 42
Willow Bank House 14, 63
Wrigglesworth, Howard family 64-65
Wrigglesworth School 11
Wright, Harry family 56-57
Wynston, A. L. family 40

Y
Young, Charles 18, 28
Young, James 5, 28

ACKNOWLEDGEMENTS

F. Alcott • H. Anderson • J. Arnold • Col. J. Barber • H. Barnhill • Rev. P. Barrow • G. Beardmore • J. Bender • E. Beeney • G. Benton • W. Biehn • W. Bradley • B. Brain • F. Brain • G. Brigden • F. Brooks • K. Brooks • T. Brown • J. Buck • J. Carter • K. B. Case • J. Cleave • P. Cleave • H. Coles • B. Cox • S. Cox • A. Currie • A. Dayfoot • K. Dills • W. Donaldson • M. Douglas • L. Duby • A. Early • G. Farnell • D. Fleishman • R. Forster • M. Foster • K. Gastle • L. D. Gowdy • W. Graham • J. Hambley • B. Harding • G. Henderson • R. Heslop • R. Heslop Jr. • T. Hill • D. Hillock • N. Holt • H. James • C. Kentner • J. King • W. Kirkwood • K. C. Lindsay • W. Lawson • J. MacFarlane • J. Mackenzie • S. Mackenzie • A. Mann • C. Martin • G. McGilvray • S.Muddle • J. Murray • M. Neilson • D. Penrice • J. Prucyk • J. Reed • M. Reed • C. Reid • M. Rowe • Rev. R. Ruggle • H. Savings • P. Saxe • M. Shepherd • B. Shoemaker • H. Shorthill • S. Silver • C. Snyder • A. Speight • M. Sunnucks • M. Taylor • C. Vale • N. Wheeler • T. Williams • B. Willoughby • N. Wilson